THE
EVERYDAY
WARRIOR

THE

A No-Hack, Practical

EVERYDAY

Approach to Life

WARRIOR

MIKE SARRAILLE

LIONCREST
PUBLISHING

COPYRIGHT © 2023 MIKE SARRAILLE

THE EVERYDAY WARRIOR
A No-Hack, Practical Approach to Life

ISBN 978-1-5445-3128-1   *Hardcover*

978-1-5445-3127-4   *Paperback*

978-1-5445-3126-7   *Ebook*

978-1-5445-3855-6   *Audiobook*

CONTENTS

Not for us alone are we born; our country, our friends, have a share in us.

—CICERO, DE OFFICIIS 1:22

This book is dedicated to all the warriors I've ever known and those I'm yet to meet—warriors in the traditional sense and in their approach to life. The extraordinary men and women I've had the honor of serving alongside in the military and private sector have made me the man I am today. I'm deeply thankful for their faith in me and commitment to coaching, mentoring, and pushing me to my limits so that I could learn, reflect, and grow.

I am grateful for all the warriors I've known. However, the risks of war vastly outweigh those found in the private sector—the loss of life versus the loss of capital. The men and women who fight their hearts out on battlefields far from home, especially those who make the ultimate sacrifice, risk everything for their beliefs. The most virtuous thing any of us can do is hold our ground for something we believe in and, if necessary, selflessly give our lives in its defense.

While serving, I watched in awe as those around me demonstrated selfless valor on a nightly basis, knowing all too well that I'd barely earned the right to share the battlefield with them. I watched how these individuals worked, trained, and lived their lives as fathers and mothers, brothers and sisters, and sons and daughters. They were warriors in the truest sense of the word. Simply being around them taught me the meaning of discipline, accountability, and how to make the seemingly impossible possible, even when the decks are stacked against you.

Sadly, many people have the wrong impression of veterans because of Hollywood's history of misrepresenting the community and the handful of veterans beating their chests in public. The reality is true warriors don't need to act like tough guys; they understand that choosing actions over words (doing > talking) allows them to speak volumes. They stay in the shadows, never bragging about how tough they are, how many medals they've earned, or how many people they've killed. In fact, the most lethal warriors I know are also the most empathetic, respectful, and humble. People naturally gravitate toward them because of what they stand for, what they do, and how they inspire those around them—including me. So, this book is dedicated to them, my raison d'être. As such, 25% of the first year's profits from the book will go to help the Special Operations Warrior Foundation provide an education for the children of fallen Special Operations soldiers. Learn more about the incredible work this nonprofit organization does at https://specialops.org.

Throughout the book, I will share the stories of some of the warriors I've had the privilege to know. I hope their stories touch your life as much as these incredible individuals have impacted mine, and the lessons they've bestowed help you reach your full potential and live a more fulfilling, purpose-driven life as an Everyday Warrior.

PREFACE

There's nothing more powerful than a humble person
with a warrior spirit who is driven by a bigger purpose.

—JEFF OSTERMAN

SINCE RETIRING FROM THE MILITARY, I'VE HAD THE OPPOR-
tunity to speak with people from across the country. Time and
again, they tell me that daily responsibilities make it difficult to
focus on personal growth, and they ask me for tips on achieving
their goals and living a happier, more fulfilling life. Sadly, this
is so prevalent that many feel compelled to take shortcuts to
attain health, wellness, and success—only to be disappointed.

After a while, I began reflecting on my time in the military and
the business world. I thought about the struggles I'd faced, the
obstacles I'd overcome, and those who helped me continue
fighting, both on and off the battlefield. Inspired by their selflessness, I combined my experiences as a Navy SEAL, the

lessons of my mentors, and what I'd learned as an entrepreneur to develop the Everyday Warrior mindset. This approach to living promotes balance and gives people the tools needed to achieve their goals and live a life that would make anybody proud. As you will read in the coming chapters, success begins with knowing yourself, finding your tribe, and understanding that failure is essential to success. I highlight these principles throughout the book with stories of people overcoming obstacles, roadblocks, and failures to accomplish extraordinary things. Along with depicting the resiliency of the human spirit, these accounts provide proof that no matter who you are, where you start, or what you're facing, you have the power to define your success, because an Everyday Warrior exists in you. I want to set the tone for this journey with an incredible tale of perseverance, drive, and commitment.

On a mid-September evening, a young family walked together through the city. The man was a surgeon, and the woman devoted much of her time to charitable causes, but nothing brought them more joy than raising their eight-year-old son. As they walked along enjoying the unseasonably warm weather, a man approached them and demanded money at gunpoint. They handed over their cash and jewelry without hesitation, but that wasn't enough—the man fired two shots at point-blank range, killing the couple instantly. The police arrived several minutes later to find the boy inconsolable, hugging his mother's body so tight that it took two officers to pull him away. With no other relatives, a family friend stepped in to raise the child. As you can imagine, life was not easy. He suffered severe PTSD, struggled with depression, and endured relentless bullying at school. As he grew, the tragedy motivated him to pursue a career in private law enforcement; he wanted to help prevent the type of senseless violence that took his parents. Years later, his hard work and dedication paid off as the city enjoyed a dramatic decrease in crime under his watch. He was so effective that the police commissioner would often invite him to consult on particularly tough cases by using a commercial-grade searchlight to blast the silhouette of a bat into the night sky.

Of course, many of you may be shaking your head. Yes, this is Batman's origin story. So, why am I telling it? As I said earlier, there's a warrior in each of us, but that doesn't mean we will all be a warrior. That's a choice we must make for ourselves. After experiencing such trauma, Bruce Wayne could have easily surrendered to his pain, blamed the world for his failures, and wasted his life making excuses. Instead, he used it as fuel to achieve his goals and make a difference for the greater good. The DC Comics team of Bob Kane and Bill Finger took their inspiration for Batman from Sherlock Holmes, a sketch by Leonardo da Vinci, and true stories of people persevering in the face of overwhelming challenges and tragedy—the types of stories movies are based on.

Some will read the true stories in this book and search for any excuse as to why it couldn't be them. They'll point to physical differences between themselves and those in the stories or claim that their success was given, not earned. Regardless of the excuses people make in life, there's a common theme: success is always beyond their control. If it weren't, they'd have to admit they're the only ones responsible for their current situation. Being an Everyday Warrior means holding yourself accountable to a higher standard, taking the difficult path, and recommitting to it daily. But it also means reaping the rewards of living a fulfilling life of purpose, impact, and balance—a trade that's well worth it.

Before we get to work, take a moment to reflect on the words of American entrepreneur Jim Rohn: "Successful people do what unsuccessful people are not willing to do. Don't wish it were easier; wish you were better." As an Everyday Warrior, be thankful that things aren't easy, because the struggles you overcome along the way help define who you are, build character, and make success more meaningful.

INTRODUCTION

Life itself is a war, and each day a battle. Fight or submit—it's entirely up to you.

SOME MAY HANDLE THE BATTLES OF LIFE BETTER THAN others, but it's not easy for anyone—it's not supposed to be. The best we can do is pursue a life of balance and purpose, but even this path is fraught with hardship. It requires always pushing yourself further, demonstrating discipline in an undisciplined world, remaining accountable even when no one is watching, and seeking to have a positive impact on those around you.

It doesn't matter who you are, where you're from, or what you've accomplished—the journey won't be easy. So, remember two things when you're struggling with doubt: nobody's perfect, and we're *all* battling something.

The single mom working two jobs to selflessly provide her children with a better life.

The entrepreneur pursuing his dreams of building a company that revolutionizes an industry.

The man who's dealing with an emotionally debilitating divorce.

The busy parent balancing the pressures of work, family, and staying healthy.

The veteran who's reestablishing her sense of identity after leaving the military.

The high school athlete who's practicing in the months leading up to his varsity tryouts.

The young professional who's struggling with depression while building his career.

The elderly volunteer fighting every day to improve her community.

The person feeling lost who knows something is missing but can't figure out what.

No matter what you're facing or who you are, you're fighting for a better life, and it's a life that you deserve.

Who's standing in your way? Despite what people in today's culture of victimhood and entitlement say, very few battles are against external forces or other people. The overwhelming majority of our failures and shortcomings are the result of internal struggles, which means the person looking back at you in the mirror each morning is also the one standing in your way.

Now the question is: are you going to take the easy route by playing the victim...

...or are you going to fight?

THE EVERYDAY WARRIOR PHILOSOPHY

Everything in life requires work—whether that's your career, physical fitness, relationships, or mental health. This effort feels easy when things run smoothly, but that never lasts. Despite our best intentions, the circumstances of life often derail us from our goals. Very few people are fortunate enough to have been taught the framework or to have developed the discipline required to remain focused when times get tough.

Today's world is under attack by those looking to take advantage of other people's insecurities and busy schedules. Besides taking cover behind the deafening noise and endless bombardment of information that defines our culture, these individuals wield an incredibly potent weapon: false promises.

Tell me if any of these sound familiar:

- Take this pill and lose fifteen pounds in just fifteen days.

- Invest now and become financially independent overnight.

- Buy this app to be more productive and successful.

- Follow this simple life hack to find true happiness.

Here's the problem: quick fixes don't work, and shortcuts are dead ends. They prevent us from developing the positive habits and discipline needed to grow. They harm us physically, mentally, and spiritually, and waste our time—the one thing we can't do if we're to achieve our goals.

If you want to live a life of purpose, there are no hacks, no silver bullets, no shortcuts. What remains is you putting in the work and driving toward your goals, one step ATTA time.

Everyday Warrior is a philosophy based on the belief that personal growth is a lifelong journey—not a destination. It's a mindset built on lessons I've learned from some of the most inspirational and highest-performing individuals in the world. This book will help you develop the warrior mindset needed to fight your battles, achieve your goals, and pursue balance in your life.

I should warn you now that this is far from a quick fix. Instead, it's a no-hack, practical framework using time-tested principles for living a good life. While the path may be long and the journey hard, success is only possible when we focus on our whole self, including the physical, mental, and spiritual.

Whether you acknowledge it or not, life is the ultimate battlefield, and it requires a warrior's mindset and strategic approach. You will face challenges that you must overcome, take on fights that bring you closer to achieving your goal, taste sweet victory, and experience the bitterness of defeat. While life is a battle, it shouldn't be viewed as a competition you can objectively win or lose, but rather a journey of learning, growth, and hopefully balance.

It is relatively easy to identify when the battle is not going your way. Here are a few signs:

- You've achieved success but still feel something's missing (purpose, joy, impact).

- You haven't set goals or are fighting for something that doesn't matter to you.

- You feel alone and lack a tribe—a sense of homecoming and belonging.

- You're experiencing self-induced stress, anxiety, and/or depression.

- You're not making progress toward achieving your goals.

- People in your life seem frustrated with you.

- You don't know what you're fighting for.

- You feel overwhelmed.

If these sound all too familiar, it's okay. These are normal setbacks that we all experience from time to time. I know because I've personally had each happen to me, sometimes several at once. They may be common, but that doesn't make them acceptable. Why? Because you deserve better and deserve to be happy. The good news is that you are in control of both. After all, you're the hero of your own story, and it's an inspirational one—even if you are still writing it.

STANDING ON THE SHOULDERS OF GIANTS

Sir Isaac Newton is among the most consequential scientists, mathematicians, and philosophers in history. His contributions to humanity forever changed the world, including the law of universal gravity, calculus, and the modern telescope. While brilliant, he knew the credit wasn't his alone, saying, "If I have seen further, it is by standing on the shoulders of giants." This simple yet profound metaphor is incredibly personal to me. Any success I've enjoyed in life is because of the men and women who've shaped, mentored, and guided me. Not only did these giants stand alongside me, but they allowed me the honor of standing upon their shoulders.

I served as a Recon Marine, Scout-Sniper, and U.S. Navy SEAL during my career. After twenty years in Special Operations, including with the elite Joint Special Operations Command (JSOC), I retired and started several companies. Some were successful, while others were the textbook definition of failures.

My military and business experience may have taught me valuable lessons about building habits, setting goals, and being a warrior, but it's not what qualifies me to write this book. That credit goes to the men and women who've encouraged, mentored, and invested in me; their wisdom humbled me, and their patience allowed me room to grow. I could never come close to fully repaying that debt, but I honor them by using their knowledge to guide your journey and by preserving their wisdom so they may live on forever in the success of future generations.

This book isn't about me—it's about you and the shoulders of those we both now stand upon.

Here are the Everyday Warrior eleven principles of living:

1. Establish the mindset of a warrior—hold yourself to high standards.

2. Embrace failure—there's no better motivator or teacher.

3. Strive for balance through mental, physical, and spiritual fitness.

4. Know thyself and continually seek self-improvement (courtesy of the U.S. Marine Corps and Army).

5. Take ownership of your life. You are not a victim.

6. Don't be a spectator; step into the arena of life. Set your intention, form a plan, and take action. Then, reflect and repeat.

7. Don't take shortcuts—they don't work! Live life one step ATTA time.

8. Learn to be comfortable being uncomfortable. Hard choices lead to an easy life.

9. The Warrior Way: Get Shit Done. Make Shit Happen. Do It All Again Tomorrow. These are the hallmarks of discipline and accountability.

10. Find your tribe. Make sure they aspire to be great— iron sharpens iron.

11. Learn to honestly critique yourself, and take time to rest, reflect, and grow.

No matter who you are or where you're from, following these principles and internalizing the Everyday Warrior mindset will give you the framework for a life of purpose, impact, and fulfillment.

ARE YOU READY?

This book alone won't change your life, nor will any other book, seminar, mentor, or coach. Their guidance may provide a framework for progress, but it can never replace action. Only one thing in this world can change your life: *you*. In the end, change is nothing more than a mindset that chooses action over complacency.

The strategies in this book are no secret. They're proven, time-tested principles that you may have even heard before. However, learning about something and living it are two very different things. Books can provide the tools, but it's up to you to use those tools to build the life you deserve. Of course, that's easier said than done—or else there wouldn't be countless self-help books published each year and even more people lining up to buy them.

AFTER ACTION REVIEWS

To facilitate your leap from reading to action, I've included an after action review (AAR) at the end of each chapter. AARs are used in the military and private sector to review the performance of individuals, teams, and organizations. They identify strengths, weaknesses, and the steps necessary for improvement.

In this book, each AAR is a structured writing and reflection exercise that will help you reflect, define your goals, and apply the principles you learn to your own journey. AARs are essential to growth and progress—so take five to ten minutes at the end of each chapter to answer the questions. I recommend writing your answers in a journal.

Your first one starts now—and I'm confident you're ready!

After Action Review

While striving for a life of impact and purpose is a never-ending journey, it most certainly has a beginning. Completing this exercise will give you a better understanding of where that is for you. There are no right or wrong answers. The most important part of this challenge is being completely honest with yourself. Vulnerability is one of the highest forms of courage.

First, answer these questions:

- Are there battles you are currently facing—or worse, have been avoiding?

- Do you believe you have room to grow and lessons to learn?

- Do you have the ability to candidly identify your strengths and weaknesses?

- Do you consider yourself disciplined and accountable for your outcomes?

- Are you willing to experience failure to leave your comfort zone and ignite personal growth?

- Are you ready to put in the work to live a more purpose-driven and fulfilling life?

If you answered yes to most of these questions, you're starting this journey from a solid position. If you answered no to most of them, take a moment to ask yourself *why*. What fears or beliefs are limiting your potential and hindering your growth? AARs and journaling are among the most powerful tools for getting at the root of an issue and identifying improvements. Give it a try and see if you can work through it. Even if you can't, I encourage you to keep reading. Just be aware that your fear, ego, or beliefs may prevent you from getting the most from this book.

Now, define your desired outcome(s). List what you'd like to achieve from reading this book and how it could potentially change your life.

Regardless of the results of your AAR, please keep an open mind as you read. At times, I may say something that you disagree with, don't think is worth trying, or even causes you to feel defensive. And that's okay. Whatever it is may not work for you, but it could also be the one thing that pushes you outside your comfort zone and changes your life.

I'm not going to pretend living a life of purpose and balance is easy because it's not. The book is called *Everyday Warrior*, not *Everyday Shortcuts to Living an Easy Life*. If that book did exist, it would be collecting dust in clearance bins across the country. The framework I lay out in the coming pages and chapters will require you to dig deep, but it will be worth it because you're not only capable of achieving it—you also deserve it, if you're willing to work for it.

1

EVERYDAY WARRIOR MINDSET

The successful warrior is the average man with laser-like focus.

—BRUCE LEE

ADAM BROWN WAS AN INCREDIBLE PERSON, A GREAT WARRIOR, AND one of the most resilient Navy SEALs I've ever had the privilege to serve alongside. His path to becoming a SEAL wasn't without adversity. Before the military, Adam battled drug addiction and had numerous brushes with the law. Still, he found it within himself to fight through and join the Navy in an attempt to better his life.

After basic training, Adam's focus shifted to becoming a Navy SEAL. He began Basic Underwater Demolition/SEAL (BUD/S) training, the world's most formidable military training program with an attrition rate as high as 90%. He demonstrated world-class mental toughness, resiliency, and perseverance to become one of the few to make it through the training and earn the title SEAL. However, Adam's military career was fraught with injuries and adversity.

During a training mishap, he was blinded in the right eye, which disabled his peripheral vision. He worked tirelessly adapting to his new circumstances, teaching himself to shoot using his nondominant eye.

Then in 2005, a convoy accident in Afghanistan left Adam's hand crushed and mangled. Although tragic, it made something very clear: Adam had no quit in him and always found a way to stay in the fight. He faced many hardships in life, and this one was no different. He pushed forward with the recovery while preparing to try out for a highly selective and specialized SEAL team. Despite the odds, Adam once again proved himself by earning a spot, which put him in the top 2% of the entire SEAL community.

While deployed to the Konar Province in 2010, his team conducted a direct action mission to capture/kill a senior Al Qaeda leader in a remote enemy stronghold deep in the Hindu Kush mountains. Once Adam's team surrounded the objective, the outnumbered SEAL and Ranger element began taking automatic weapons fire and rocket-propelled grenades from enemy positions throughout the valley. With the intensity of the firefight increasing, Adam boldly assumed a position that he knew would make him vulnerable but would also provide the best chance of eliminating a group of enemy fighters. This incredible act of bravery cost Adam his life. He was posthumously awarded the Silver Star, the nation's third-highest award for valor.

A true warrior, Adam faced his battles with courage and never viewed himself as a victim. He decided what he wanted, fought for it, and kept moving forward—that is a warrior mindset. You may not have known who Adam Brown was before today, but now I hope you'll never forget him. To learn more about Adam, the biography *Fearless: The Undaunted Courage and Ultimate Sacrifice of Navy SEAL Team SIX Operator Adam Brown,* by Eric Blehm, memorialized his story.

WHAT IS A WARRIOR?

At this point, you might be wondering how you could ever identify as a warrior if you're not even in the profession of arms.

Being a warrior has nothing to do with your profession and everything to do with your mindset!

We often relegate the title of *warrior* to professional soldiers, namely those in the military. While *warrior* and *soldier* are not mutually exclusive, I can assure you that not all soldiers are warriors—a distinction that took me far too long to recognize. The military consists of two types of soldiers: warriors and warfighters. Warfighters are capable soldiers who possess physical courage and train in the art of war, but the greatest soldiers I've known had warrior blood pumping through their veins. They demonstrated unmatched discipline, accountability, and not just physical courage, but moral courage. There's no shortage of physical courage in the military. Moral courage, however, is a rare occurrence that few have the fortitude to display. Men and women with moral courage are prepared to step forward and make the ultimate sacrifice for a cause they deem righteous. Their courage sets them apart as world-class warriors, part of an elite few.

The difference between warriors and warfighters is an age-old concept. Heraclitus, an Ionian philosopher in ancient Greece, wrote, "Out of every one hundred men, ten shouldn't even be there, eighty are just targets, nine are the real fighters, and we are lucky to have them, for they make the battle. But [out of the hundred], one is a warrior, and he will bring the others back."

Here are a few characteristics warriors share:

- Warriors hold themselves to a higher standard.

- Warriors dedicate themselves to living virtuous and impactful lives.

- Warriors have a moral compass and the moral courage to do what is right, no matter the consequences.

- Warriors understand that the pursuit of balance and knowledge is a lifelong journey.

- Warriors do not fear failure; they understand they must accept risk to experience growth.

- Warriors accept that they don't have all the answers and take every opportunity to learn from those around them—especially from those they disagree with.

- Warriors adapt and overcome—no matter the size of the obstacle.

- Warriors *never* quit.

- Warriors are always positive, kind, and respectful. They seek to give more than they take and understand that leading by example lights the path for others to follow.

- Warriors hold themselves accountable and refuse to accept the victimhood mentality spreading through modern society.

Everyone has the potential to become a warrior, but they must first have a cause to defend. According to John Stuart Mill, a nineteenth-century English philosopher, "A man who has nothing for which he is willing to fight, nothing which is more important than his own personal safety, is a miserable creature and has no chance of being free unless made and kept so by the exertions of better men than himself."

In other words, if you don't accept your battles and you refuse to defend what is right—whether out of laziness, self-preservation, or lack of confidence—then you relinquish control of your destiny. Life is brutal enough without acquiescing control of it to other people.

When we think of warriors, people like Adam Brown come to mind. We most often hear the word *warrior* used in the context of those willing to sacrifice themselves for others, but the term has a much broader meaning, one that has nothing to do with armed conflict and everything to do with living a virtuous life. Everyday Warriors exist in every profession, culture, and facet of life, from the volunteer serving his community to the single mom selflessly working to provide her children with the life she never had. Unlike the classic warrior, they are not armed or trained in the art of war, yet they wield a powerful weapon: the Everyday Warrior mindset.

WHAT IS THE WARRIOR MINDSET?

High-performing individuals often use the phrase "mindset is everything." Your mindset is your attitude toward life and the lens through which you view the world. When challenges or opportunities arise, your mindset determines how you respond and react.

With a warrior mindset, you begin to consider challenges and problems as the basis for opportunity and ownership. Cultivating a warrior mindset means accepting that each day will be tough but knowing that you can overcome anything. It means embracing the journey and focusing on becoming the best version of yourself.

We each face unique challenges and circumstances. No matter the battle, Everyday Warriors share several key traits that define their mindset and help them succeed.

Drive

In *The Talent War: How Special Operations and Great Organizations Win on Talent,* I wrote about drive—the unrelenting need for achievement and self-improvement. Driven individuals want to be the best, grow, and push themselves. They're willing to take risks and seek new achievements. Drive is essentially our ability to identify what is worth fighting for; without it, we lack a sense of purpose. While you may not always get to choose your battles, you do have a choice in how you fight. So, when you do decide to fight, have the dedication, desire, and drive to see it through and be the very best version of yourself.

Positivity

You're statistically more likely to receive a favorable outcome if you approach a situation with positivity. Positivity breeds self-belief, and when you believe in yourself, you build confidence and self-esteem. In other words, positivity attracts positivity, and negativity breeds negativity.

Even in dire circumstances, positivity can go a long way. A situation might appear impossible, but letting it devolve into negativity isn't going to help. However, positivity can. I remember being in firefights—outnumbered and exhausted—when one of the SEALs would crack a joke. The worst possible time for a joke, right? Not at all. Bringing positivity and levity into this stressful situation helped us refocus our energy and get our minds right. This little bit of laughter made us realize that we had this, and that's when we'd bring the fight to the enemy.

Rich Diviney, retired Navy SEAL commander and author of *The Attributes*, points out, "Sense of humor isn't just a tool you can utilize to make tough times easier. Knowing how to find joy in every situation you're in is as good for you...physically as it is mentally." Remember, life isn't something you win but rather something you seek to do well. Positivity will help you live well even as you fight your battles.

Humble Confidence

Humble confidence is a concept I've embraced over the last few years as I've reflected on my time in Special Operations. The most elite warriors don't tout their accomplishments, tell you how tough they are or even how many medals they've earned. Instead, they have confidence in their abilities while understanding that there's always room for improvement and that they can learn from others' experience and knowledge.

Humble confidence is essential. I'm rarely the most intelligent person in the room, nor do things come easily to me. But while I'm wildly flawed and imperfect, I'm confident that no matter the challenge, large or small, I can overcome it—and with the right mindset, you will too. Even if things don't work out the way you expect, you'll have the confidence to know there are other paths forward and the humility to recognize there's more you must learn to make them a reality.

Resiliency

Resiliency is managing challenges, shortfalls, and hardships while quickly recovering and learning from your experiences. Adam's story is a master class in resiliency. He overcame addiction, losing an eye, and then severely injuring his right hand. Despite those around him advising against it, he continued and finished his SEAL training, pushing forward and succeeding on the highest, most competitive level possible.

You may be at the beginning, middle, or nearing the end of a lifelong battle. Despite where you are in life, battles change over time. Some days may not feel like a battle, while others feel like everything's exploding around you. Resiliency is picking yourself up after getting knocked down and knowing that even if you do everything right, you won't always win. It's the most significant factor separating the SEAL candidates who complete BUD/S and the more than 90% who quit. Those who make it are examples of what resiliency can help achieve in life.

Growth-Minded

In her book *Mindset,* psychologist Carol Dweck identifies two fundamental mindsets that impact success: a fixed mindset and a growth mindset. A fixed mindset is the belief that our talents and traits are *fixed,* meaning they are innate gifts we have at birth. You're either smart or not, talented or not, a good communicator or not, and so on. On the other hand, those with a growth mindset believe that we develop abilities through dedication and hard work. A growth mindset is about continuous improvement, whereas a fixed mindset is about not trying because you're powerless to change. As you can imagine, the latter can crush one's drive to improve.

Dweck's research found that those with a growth mindset achieve far greater outcomes than those with a fixed mindset. In school, business, sports, relationships, and more, a growth mindset is an early indicator of success. It discourages self-imposed limits and allows you to see failure as an opportunity to learn rather than a weakness.

Action-Oriented

The United States Marine Corps and United States Army ensure those in its ranks develop a critical trait they call a "bias for action," more commonly known as being *action-oriented*. When facing uncertainty, many people feel that doing nothing is the safest choice. Not Marines, soldiers, or Everyday Warriors; they know how to assess the situation, evaluate the circumstances, and take the appropriate action. General George Patton famously said, "A good plan, violently executed now, is better than a perfect plan next week." He believed in using the best information available to make a plan, then executing it with immediacy and commitment. When choosing between action and inaction—doing and not doing—an Everyday Warrior acts.

One caveat is that just because you *can* act doesn't mean you *should*. It's not always necessary to take swift action, seize every opportunity, or solve every problem. Sometimes restraint is the right option, as it gives you a chance to gather more information. Senior enlisted advisors in the SEALs taught me that while some problems are significant enough to warrant immediate attention, others are not and will solve themselves given time. The key is learning to tell the difference. You do that by *responding*, not just reacting. Instead of immediately jumping into action, take a tactical knee and assess the situation. Showing restraint is akin to taking action, as long as it's a conscious, intentional choice instead of a way to ignore or avoid a problem.

The alternative to being action-oriented is experiencing paralysis through analysis, getting stuck thinking about a problem instead of taking action. Usually, this happens due to a fear of risk or failure. To become action-oriented, you must accept some risks. Though you won't always know the outcome, you must act. Nobody wants to be on their deathbed saying, "Damn, I wish I had taken more risks and gone for it."

I'm not saying to take needless risks but calculated ones. There's no reward without risk, and living to the fullest means embracing the ones that push us toward our goals. It all comes down to a famous saying that few truly understand: You only get one life. Live it to the fullest.

Accountability and Discipline

Has anybody ever told you to *own it*? This common military expression is one that I heard a lot in my non-military house growing up. Ownership is recognizing you are not a victim and owning your choices instead of blaming circumstances or other people. The two keys of ownership are self-accountability and self-discipline. Self-accountability is holding yourself responsible rather than relying on others to do so. Self-discipline is using internal motivations to regulate your behavior rather than depending on external motivations. Having both is how you get shit done and make shit happen.

Those who refuse to hold themselves accountable will never learn from their mistakes. We have a proud tradition in our country of promoting accountability and teaching our children the importance of ownership. These values are the antithesis of the victimhood and entitlement mindsets currently metastasizing through our nation.

Self-Reflection

Self-reflection is the disciplined act of assessing ourselves and our current position in life. It is about giving serious thought to our actions and motives so that we can make the necessary adjustments to become better, more impactful individuals. Reflection requires that we take an honest and objective look at ourselves—our thoughts, feelings, and actions—with an interest and curiosity that allows for growth. After all, we should be our own worst critics.

A common thread among the high performers I've worked with is their reflective nature. They all look back on their successes and failures to extract lessons and grow. For most of them, this process includes journaling. Reflection keeps them focused on their goals and continual improvement.

Vulnerability

You might not associate vulnerability with warriors, but in Special Operations, vulnerability and emotional intimacy are core strengths. In fact, they are *requirements,* because on the battlefield you must be able to trust the soldier next to you with your life. Only through vulnerability can you achieve total trust—both in others and in yourself.

Instinctually, we want to hide our weaknesses and avoid anything with the potential to be harmful or embarrassing. While building emotional walls keeps the bad things out, it also becomes a prison of your own making. Acknowledging hard truths and opening yourself up to others is uncomfortable, but it's the only way to grow.

Pragmatism

Pragmatism is approaching your life and problems in a reasonable, logical way. It's allowing facts and experience to guide your decisions. Dare greatly and embrace risk, but be pragmatic in how you set out to achieve your goals.

It's a marathon, not a sprint—still, make sure your laces are tied tight. Understand that success is not a straight line and may require a thousand micro-goals. Being slow, steady, and pragmatic is how you achieve lasting results and develop lifelong habits.

HOW TO BUILD A WARRIOR MINDSET

You may not have a warrior mindset yet, but that's okay: it's not set in stone. While mindset is everything, it's also a choice. We are who we choose to be. Let me say that again: *we are who we choose to be*. Never allow anyone else to define who you are and who you aren't.

Building a warrior mindset happens through small, iterative steps. Want to be more resilient? The next time you face a setback, choose to get back up and keep fighting. Want more positivity in your life? Find something to be grateful for. Want to develop humble confidence? When you think you know everything, keep an open mind to learning from others.

Developing a warrior mindset takes time, dedication, and hard work. It's thousands of small choices. At first, you may have to consciously work at it, but the more you practice, the more natural it'll become, until it's a habit.

Remember, being a warrior is a way of life, not a profession. It's being prepared to tackle challenges as they arise and seizing opportunities as they present themselves. If you develop a strong warrior mindset, your perspective and life will change for the better.

The sooner you develop a warrior mindset, the more prepared you will be for periods of volatility, uncertainty, and chaos. Not only will you survive...you'll thrive. Take the Everyday

Warrior pledge, and start developing this warrior mindset today, not tomorrow:

> I pledge to strive for progress instead of perfection, develop a bias for action, and never stop pursuing potential. I commit to a lifelong journey of personal growth and acknowledge that lasting change requires time and consistency—not hacks and shortcuts. I accept that failure is a part of the process and that we learn more from our struggles than our successes. I will fall, but I pledge to always get back up, regroup, and continue moving forward. I will do my best to inspire others through my actions, compassion, and vulnerability—because I am an Everyday Warrior.

After Action Review

• Do you possess a warrior mindset? Why or why not?

• Rank yourself on the warrior attributes, from strongest to weakest. Then explain why you consider each to be a strength or a weakness. Ask a trusted friend or family member to rank you, then compare results.

   * Drive

   * Positivity

* Humble confidence

* Resiliency

* Growth-minded

* Action-oriented

* Accountability and discipline

* Self-reflection

* Vulnerability

* Pragmatism

Key Takeaways

- Being a warrior isn't about being a soldier. It's about your *mindset* and holding yourself to high standards.

- A warrior mindset is approaching life with drive, positivity, humble confidence, resiliency, growth-mindedness, action orientation, ownership, self-reflection, vulnerability, and pragmatism.

- Your mindset is a choice, built through thousands of tiny everyday decisions.

2

FAILURE: LIFE'S GREATEST MENTOR

I've missed more than 9,000 shots in my career. I've lost almost 300 games. 26 times I've been trusted to take the game-winning shot and missed. I've failed over and over and over again in my life. And that is why I succeed.

—MICHAEL JORDAN

IN 1980, SHORTLY AFTER THEIR FOUNDING, DELTA FORCE launched Operation Eagle Claw, a watershed moment for the Special Operations community. The mission was catastrophic: the team failed to rescue the fifty-two Americans held hostage during the Iran Hostage Crisis. Tragically, eight service members lost their lives when a C-130 transport aircraft collided with a helicopter. Understandably, all involved felt demoralized.

The Delta Force team returned to Oman to regroup. British contractors stationed at the same airport pieced together what had happened from watching the news. They delivered a case of beer to the team with a brief note scribbled on a scrap of cardboard: "To you all, from us all, for having the guts to try."

That operation is now considered the most successful failed Special Operations mission in history. Many of the procedures and tactics that are now commonplace in Special Operations emerged from the lessons gleaned during that mission. While that failure was their first, it would be far from their last. Since 1980, they've failed more than a thousand times in training and combat. Nonetheless, they've become recognized as the world's premier special operations unit—not despite their failures, but because of them. A successful organization doesn't define itself by avoiding failure entirely, but rather by how it responds when failure occurs. For Delta Force, every defeat was a lesson in becoming more capable, lethal, and effective in defending their nation and eradicating evil.

That scrap of cardboard left by British contractors over forty years ago is still proudly displayed at a Special Operations unit. It captures a core tenet of the U.S. Special Operations ethos: always have the guts—a.k.a., courage—to try. While falling short of our goals is terrifying, the only failures are those who've never failed—because that means they've never tried.

FAILURE DOES NOT MEAN LOSING

It may seem strange to talk about failure so early, before we've even really started. But you need to go into this journey prepared for it, because failing is unavoidable. You will fail, which is good since no greater mentor exists. While failure carries a negative connotation, Everyday Warriors understand that success and failure are not the same as winning and losing. Failure is all about learning. The hard lessons learned through failure are some of life's most valuable, and while success builds confidence, failure builds character.

How you handle failure is one of the most significant predictors of success. The Special Operations selection process pushes applicants to the edge of failure to test their response. Some people won't get up after being pushed down five times. That choice may seem insignificant at the time, but it tells instructors all they need to know about someone's mindset. The Special Operations community knows failure is inevitable, so they need people who will get back up a sixth, seventh, and hundredth time as if their life depends on it—because eventually, it will.

I'm thankful for all the times I've failed; those experiences helped me build resiliency and intestinal fortitude. I've never been the strongest, the fastest, the most intelligent, or the most articulate. Instead, I had to work through my failures and strengthen my weaknesses.

Everyone who's attained any level of success has experienced failure. Failing keeps us humble and forces us to improve until we make it, boosting our determination and confidence. It is the refining fire by which persistence becomes success.

THE TRILLION-DOLLAR COACH
TAKES ON FAILURE

Thanks to incredible mentors, I've come to recognize the beauty and value of failure. One such person was the legendary "trillion-dollar coach" Bill Campbell. An incredible man, Bill served as director of the board at Apple, CEO of Claris, Intuit, and GO Corporation, and an executive coach for Silicon Valley's most elite leaders. I had the privilege of meeting Bill, and he shared this story about his time at Intuit.

A senior executive had pursued a new venture, but the launch was disastrous. Bill called a mandatory meeting; everyone, including the person behind the venture, assumed they were there for a public firing. Instead, Bill turned the failure into a teachable moment and applauded the executive's effort by saying, "I know it didn't work out the way you intended, but the lessons we've learned will make this organization stronger. Now, we reset and give it another shot." By showing the value of failure,

Bill dramatically shifted the company culture and gave employees the confidence to take calculated risks. His decision to be a leader, instead of a "boss," paid off in innovation, loyalty, and success. This story is an example of how our approach to failure impacts those around us. So, whether it's as a leader, a parent, or just a human being, ask yourself: what lessons on failure do I want to teach?

FEELINGS OF FAILURE: INSIDE AND OUT

Nobody likes failure. It hits hard on three levels: practical, internal, and external. On a practical level, failure sets us back from our goals and can have damaging consequences, like the loss of money or opportunity. Internally, failure is a blow to our ego and demoralizing to our mental and spiritual selves, often causing feelings of shame and guilt.

Often, our biggest fear regarding failure doesn't stem from the practical or the internal—but rather the external. Failure can make us feel that our credibility is damaged, cause us to fixate on what others think, and have a devastating effect on how we perceive ourselves.

For many, the most challenging part of failing is showing vulnerability. There's a stigma attached to failure, which often carries an unfounded fear of judgment. How would you react if a friend openly discussed their failures? Would you think less of them? Or would you appreciate their honesty and applaud their risk?

Of course, not everyone is supportive and understanding. The world is full of people who will judge you, whether you succeed or fail. Forget them; negativity is all they have. On April 23, 1910, former President Theodore Roosevelt addressed this very topic during *Citizenship in a Republic*, more famously known as his "The Man in the Arena" speech:

> It is not the critic who counts; not the man who points out how the strong man stumbles, or where the doer of deeds could have done them better. The credit belongs to the man who is actually in the arena, whose face is marred by dust and sweat and blood; who strives valiantly; who errs, who comes short again and again, because there is no effort without error and shortcoming; but who does actually strive to do the deeds; who knows great enthusiasms, the great devotions; who spends himself in a worthy cause; who at the best knows in the end the triumph of high achievement, and who at the worst, if he fails, at least fails while daring greatly, so that his place shall never be with those cold and timid souls who neither know victory nor defeat.

Far too many people in this world are so busy protecting themselves from what *might* happen that they miss out on what *could* happen. That is true failure. As an Everyday Warrior, find the courage to step up, dare greatly, and show vulnerability, even in the face of failure.

SUCCESS IS RARELY A STRAIGHT LINE

When you look back at someone's life, it's easy to connect the dots and craft a linear narrative: X, then Y, led to Z. The reality is that success is rarely a straight line; it's filled with plenty of ups and downs.

I was the only one in my class not to graduate high school on time, and my first try at college was short-lived. I was essentially kicked out of the University of Colorado's Naval ROTC program. They said that I didn't have what it takes for the military, never mind a career in Special Operations. So, what did I do? I enlisted in the Marine Corps, became a Recon Marine, a Scout-Sniper, and attained the rank of sergeant before the military sent me back to college to finish my degree and receive my commission. I graduated from Texas A&M University with a 3.6 GPA before going through BUD/S and becoming a Navy SEAL. I had many successes and failures as a SEAL, but I ultimately made it to the Tier One level. Since then, I've finished my MBA and started multiple businesses. It may have been an indirect, haphazard journey filled with twists and turns, but it was my path.

Your path to success will not always be straightforward. As you're navigating through that tough terrain, remember that failure is just a step in the process, not the end of your journey. Often, it's the beginning of something great. With focus and resilience, you'll arrive where you're meant to be—even if it looks completely different than you imagined.

IT'S NOT HOW YOU FAIL—IT'S HOW YOU RECOVER

Getting back up is the best response to getting knocked down, but it isn't easy. When we set ambitious goals and aim for success, it hurts when we fall short. We shouldn't expect it not to.

Although each of us has a unique process for working through failure, we all need a mechanism to deflect negativity and move toward positivity. Without it, we become stuck in emotional fallout and miss the opportunities for growth that failure provides.

To process failure, consider these steps:

- **Work through your feelings:** We all have emotions connected to failing, such as guilt, shame, embarrassment, and demoralization. Just because you recognize the value of failure doesn't mean it hurts any less. Failure has left me in the fetal position for hours, with feelings of devastation washing over me. Learning to work through those emotions is the first step to resilience. Your emotions are natural and valid, so allow yourself to have them. Ignoring them won't make them go away; they'll just simmer below the surface and explode later. Typically, shame and regret are by-products of suppressed feelings we refuse to fully process.

- **Reflect on both the negative and positive:** Take the time to find the positive in failure. Recognize what you've learned and appreciate its value. However, finding the positive does not mean being unrealistic or annoyingly optimistic. It's important to see failure from both sides. If you dismiss the negative aspects completely, you're preventing yourself from growing. Reflect on what went wrong, even if it's painful. The only way to learn from a mistake is to examine and understand it. The negative aspects of failure motivate us to change and do better in the future. Just make sure you don't get stuck in a cycle of negative thinking.

- **Be realistic about the impact:** We tend to catastrophize when we fail. Often our emotional reaction is so disproportionate to the situation or we are so hyper-focused on what others think that it inflates the failure. Take a step back and look at it objectively. What are the practical implications? Did you lose money or waste resources? Did you damage relationships? Is the impact permanent or a temporary setback? Usually, once you move past the emotions, you'll see the failure is negligible compared to what you initially thought.

- **Ask yourself what's next:** Your ultimate response to failure is what matters most. Let it overwhelm you, and you'll be so determined never to fail again that you won't even try. Take time to process the failure, but climb back on that proverbial horse as quickly as possible. Start by figuring out what steps you can take to address the damage. Next, reflect and refocus on your overall goal, make necessary adjustments to your plan, and start making forward progress.

- **Seek support:** Surround yourself with people who share a like-minded view of failure—those who will congratulate you on your attempt. They will help shift your perspective, and their relative distance from the failure means they can offer objective advice on what went wrong and what you can do differently in the future.

Knowing what to do won't make it any less painful; some failures will just haunt you. Even so, failure is not an assessment of your worth or an indictment of your ability to achieve your goals. It's never too late to learn from your failures and move forward. Press the clutch and shift from recovery into high gear. That resilience and momentum you feel rumbling under the hood are signs that you've turned failure into fuel—now hit the gas!

After Action Review

People don't typically post their failures on social media. This contributes to a self-perpetuating cycle: we only show our successes because that's all we see from other people, and they only show their successes because that's all they see from us. After years of conditioning, concealing failure out of shame feels natural. How do you break this destructive cycle? First, you do something different.

I know showing vulnerability is uncomfortable, but opening up about your failures will create a sense of community that benefits everybody. Leading a life of impact is not just about your success; it's also about your impact on others.

Film a short video talking about a failure. Explain what happened, where you think it went wrong, what you've learned, and what actions you're taking to ensure success next time.

Then replay it for yourself. I guarantee that it will be cathartic.

If you are feeling particularly courageous, share it with someone else. If you need someone to talk to, you can send it privately to me (@mr.sarraille) or to the Everyday Warrior team (@the_everydaywarrior) on Instagram. Of course, I'd never repost or share it—unless you want me to. Another option is to openly share your struggles with the community by tagging #EverydayWarrior or #OneStepATTATime. You may be surprised by the encouragement, advice, and support you receive, as well as the impact your vulnerability has. It's incredible what you can accomplish as part of a community.

Warning: Beware of the trolls, haters, and cyber-bullies. Protect yourself by ignoring and blocking the keyboard cowards who project their misery by tearing others down. Whenever someone demonstrates vulnerability and accepts the risks required to achieve greatness, those in the cheap seats will always look to criticize and diminish them. They are miserable, cowardly creatures (victims in their own minds) who lack the courage to step into the arena of life. Pray that they find the path to a challenging and rewarding life.

Key Takeaways

- Reframing the way you view failure will help you recognize its value and identify the opportunities for growth it provides. Some of life's greatest lessons stem from failure.

- Failing is a necessary step in the process of achieving success. The only way to avoid failure is by never trying to achieve your goals, which will also eliminate your chance of living a life of purpose and impact.

- Everyday Warriors recognize that failure does not define us, but our responses do. Vulnerability and reflection allow you to learn, grow, and return to an action-oriented mindset following failure.

3

THE ENDLESS PURSUIT OF BALANCE: WHOLE PERSON CONCEPT

Mens sana in corpore sano.
"A healthy mind in a healthy body."

—JUVENAL, SATIRE X, The Vanity of Human Wishes

FEW NAMES ARE AS SYNONYMOUS WITH OLYMPIC GLORY AS Michael Phelps. At seven years old, he set out on a journey that would define his life, capture the world's imagination, and shatter a record set by Leonidas from Rhodes in 152 BC. Arguably the greatest swimmer in history, Phelps appeared in his first Olympics at fifteen years old. So, how does someone so young get the opportunity to compete on the international stage? That's simple—he earned it. In just eight years, he went from a child afraid to submerge his head underwater to the youngest American male swimmer to ever compete.

His experience in Sydney only made him work harder. Then, in 2004, Phelps became a superstar when he won eight medals in Athens, Greece, including six gold. By the time he retired in 2016, he was the most successful Olympian in history, having won a total of twenty-eight medals, including twenty-three gold, thirteen of which were individual golds. While Phelps accomplished extraordinary things, he sacrificed a lot too. When other kids were enjoying their youth, he was in the pool; when his peers were experiencing life, he was in the pool; and when others were developing close bonds with friends, he was in the pool. His singular focus may have made him the best in the world, but pursuing balance would have allowed him to make his personal life as successful as his professional one.

Achieving greatness will always require us to set priorities, but it's essential we not let that focus be all consuming. Phelps appeared to have it all, but his struggles with drugs and alcohol remind us that while sacrificing balance in the pursuit of success may end in greatness, there's always a cost. Whether that's our mental, physical, or spiritual health—it's a price that's just too high to pay.

WHOLE PERSON CONCEPT

The whole person concept is a philosophical approach that bases an individual's overall health on the entirety of their being: mental (or emotional), physical, and spiritual.

Connecting mental, spiritual, and physical balance can be traced back through antiquity, from the Greek philosopher Plato's belief that "the body and mind should be cultivated together" to Roman poet Juvenal's maxim "a healthy mind in a healthy body." Greek philosophy defined a well-balanced person as someone who represented physical fitness, mental acuity, and spiritual depth. The celebration of the physical, mental, and spiritual is visible throughout ancient Greek culture, including in their art, the Olympic games, and their polytheistic belief system.

The whole person concept is integral to the Special Operations selection processes and to the intelligence community's ability to complete accurate security clearance assessments.

When recruiting an Army Green Beret or a Navy SEAL, we're not looking for the strongest, smartest, or fastest person. We're looking for someone who can thrive in an environment of volatility, uncertainty, complexity, and ambiguity (commonly referred to as a VUCA environment). Decades of research and experience have proven that the most effective operators are those who exemplify a balance of mental, physical, and emotional strength. These are the individuals who can regulate stress and consistently perform at the highest levels despite adverse conditions.

This idea of balance applies to Everyday Warriors just as much as it does military warriors. Each of us experiences VUCA environments during our life; if you're wondering whether or not this includes you, it does. On a national scale, we've all faced volatile, uncertain, complex, and ambiguous times, including 9/11, the 2008 financial crisis, and COVID-19. On a personal level, you've undoubtedly gone through other VUCA environments, whether it's divorce, job loss, parenthood, sickness, or any number of challenges.

Your ability to succeed in the face of hardship depends on who you are as an individual. Since being an Everyday Warrior is different than being a warrior in the classic sense, I've made slight adjustments to the whole person framework. Instead of physical, mental, and emotional, I've shifted to physical, mental, and spiritual. I feel these three pillars more closely align with the needs of modern society and will prove the most useful in helping you achieve fulfillment.

DIFFICULT BUT NECESSARY: THE BALANCING ACT OF LIFE

Life is hard—that is a fundamental truth. Full stop. There's no sugarcoating it. One of the biggest challenges we face is *time*.

Time is the most valuable resource on earth and one of the most finite. Each of us only has so many hours in a day and so many days in our life; faced with this scarcity, we sacrifice balance. We skip the gym, don't carve out time for social interactions, and work until we burn out. We prioritize success in one area of our life at the expense of all others, much like Michael Phelps did in his quest to make history.

I know it often feels like there aren't enough hours in the day, and some days you really don't have the time to care for yourself physically, mentally, and spiritually. That is the reason we will never achieve perfect balance—it doesn't exist. Even so, on a macro level, striving for balance is necessary to sustain optimal performance over time. *That's what it's all about—not peak performance, but maintaining optimal performance over days, months, years, and decades.*

While you can survive being off-balance for a while, eventually it will catch up to you in the form of health problems, insomnia, depression, and more. Pursuing balance is also critical because the pillars work in tandem with one another. For example, when you are physically fit, your body increases the amount of oxygen it sends to your brain, which improves your ability to regulate stress and creates a sense of mental and spiritual clarity. If you focus on just one pillar, you unnecessarily restrict your potential. By working on all three, you increase the level of progress that you can achieve in each one.

In life, a lack of balance limits growth. Remember: you are not just a body, a mind, or a spirit; you are all three—a whole person. If you were to only focus on your physical self, your muscles might grow, but you, in your entirety, would not. When you ignore a pillar, you don't simply stagnate; you deteriorate. So while you may temporarily make strides in one area of your life, you do so at the expense of all others. It's like taking one step forward only to take one back. In the end, where does that leave you? If this were *Jeopardy!*, the correct response would be: What is *back to where I started*? Wasting time is a setback you can't afford, and balance is what prepares you physically, mentally, and spiritually for the battles to come. Balance is your armor.

FITNESS: BODY, MIND, AND SPIRIT

Balance is not a one-time achievement, but a continual pursuit. Just like excellence, it is a lifelong journey with no final destination. For that reason, think of the three pillars in terms of fitness. When you think of fitness, your mind likely jumps to working out, but fitness is much more than that. Fitness is the state of being healthy, which not only means physical health, but mental acuity, happiness, and overall well-being. This kind of fitness is achieved and maintained over time through consistent effort, and it's something you and you alone are responsible for. As Brunello Cucinelli said, "There are three things you cannot buy. Fitness: You have to keep fit, whether you're rich or not. Diet: You cannot pay someone to be on a diet for you. Then, looking after your soul. No one can possibly treat your soul but you."

Like gaining muscle mass or losing weight, mental and spiritual fitness requires work. Muscle growth involves targeted stress, followed by rest periods (and appropriate nutrition). Neglecting that same muscle leads to atrophy, the gradual decline in the effectiveness of a muscle caused by underuse. Your mental strength and spiritual strength are no different. Let them go unattended, and atrophy sets in.

Physical Fitness

Physical fitness is the cornerstone upon which the Everyday Warrior grows mentally and spiritually. In fact, a recent study published in *The Lancet Psychiatry* found that those who regularly exercise have 1.5 fewer days impacted by poor mental health each month. Yet many people in the United States struggle with physical fitness. According to the Centers for Disease Control and Prevention, between 1999 and 2018, obesity in adults increased from 30.5% to 42.4%. For the first time in our nation's history, we've passed the 40% mark, which means nearly half of all adults are obese. In addition, 73.6% of Americans are overweight.

What can we do about it? First, we must understand that physical fitness is about making healthy choices, building positive habits, and pursuing progress, not perfection. I'm not recommending spending eight hours a day in the gym, depriving yourself of food, or buying products that promise instant results. Quite the opposite; extremes guarantee failure, and shortcuts don't work.

Instead of seeking shortcuts or dramatic, unrealistic changes in a short period of time, focus on making incremental changes that improve your health, increase your quality of life, and keep you motivated. If you have done damage to your body for three years with a bad diet and lack of physical fitness, I assure you it is going to take a year or two to return to your desired level of fitness. That's okay. The goal is not to train like a professional athlete. Remember: we're striving for sustained optimal performance, not *peak* performance.

Physical fitness comes down to three things:

- **Healthy diet:** You will often hear experts say that 70% to 80% of physical fitness comes down to diet. That's why gyms are filled with people who work out every day but fail to reach their desired fitness goals. They simply lack discipline in their diets. This is most commonly caused by consuming alcohol, unhealthy foods, or too much/not enough of the macronutrients (carbs, proteins, fats) our bodies require. Instead, eat a balanced diet, limit high-calorie foods, and abstain from harmful substances. I have found that drinking enough water to stay hydrated and eating four to six small, proportioned meals throughout the day allows me to maintain proper macronutrient levels and fuels my success. Do I still occasionally have a drink or enjoy dessert? Hell yes! But never to excess.

- **Exercise:** Incorporating activities that target your cardiovascular health, strength, flexibility, and bone density will improve your quality of life and general well-being. When selecting an exercise regimen, be sure to develop it around your desired fitness goals and speak with your doctor about any health concerns. There's a good chance it'll include strength training. I bring this up because there's a misconception that weight training is only for those who want to build a physique like Arnold Schwarzenegger's or Lenda Murray's. This is simply not true. The health benefits of strength training include increased bone strength, joint flexibility, and a reduced risk of sustaining age-related falls. It's important not to rule something out simply because it's unfamiliar. So, whether you're focusing on running, weight loss, or just staying healthy, choosing a balanced routine will help you reach your goals.

- **Rest:** Giving your body the time it needs to recuperate and recover from physical exertion is one of the most important things you can do for your health. I have witnessed friends fail to get adequate rest after returning to a fitness-oriented lifestyle. They're so motivated by how they feel that they end up hurting themselves from overuse injuries or exhaustion.

Although physical fitness is often associated with diet and exercise, it's also essential to monitor for acute changes in your health, get routine medical checkups, and protect yourself from injury through mobility or agility training. Along with the more traditional approaches to staying fit, proactive measures are paramount to respecting your body.

If you've neglected your health in the past, don't worry—there's no better time to start than today. Not next week, not next month, not New Year's Day. Now. I know that it's easy to put it off until tomorrow, but we both know what happens when tomorrow comes. Make the hard decision because your time is now!

Mental Fitness

Mental fitness is a state of well-being in which we realize our potential, self-worth, and resiliency. This realization leads to increased self-confidence in our ability to overcome volatile, uncertain, and chaotic situations. Mental fitness is a lifelong journey that allows us to establish and maintain a positive mindset that helps us navigate stress and enjoy life.

The persistent stigmas surrounding mental health harm countless people by shaming them away from getting the help and support they need. According to the National Alliance on Mental Illness (NAMI), in 2020, one in every five adults experienced some type of mental illness, and more than twelve million had suicidal thoughts. Mental health issues are a reality that so many people struggle with daily, and acknowledging that is a crucial step in shedding the stigma and addressing the issue. Instead of contributing to the negativity, Everyday Warriors show respect and kindness, even when others don't. We understand that growth requires us to demonstrate vulnerability and accept ourselves and others.

We should *all* be engaging in mental care. The brain is not technically a muscle, but it still requires continual exercise, conditioning, and rest. The relentless pace of life often distracts us from caring for our minds. That means we must act with intention by focusing on activities that encourage creativity, promote stimulation, and foster a sense of emotional balance. There are many ways to do this; here are a few:

- Investing just five minutes each day in meditation, focused breathing, and visualization exercises can provide a new perspective on life.

- Reading books and listening to podcasts for ten to thirty minutes a day can expose you to fresh ideas, help you discover new things, and expand your mind.

- Five to ten minutes of journaling each morning, which I call Morning Affirmations, and evening, which I refer to as Evening Reflections, is an excellent tool for maintaining a sharp mind. Transferring your thoughts to paper allows you to see your day with unbelievable clarity and makes space in your mind for new ideas.

- Speaking with a mental health professional allows you to discuss your problems and take steps to get back on track. The old military mantra of "suffer in silence" is one of the worst things you can do. True warriors are willing to be vulnerable. Asking for help and admitting that you're struggling is one of the bravest things any warrior can do, and it demonstrates the highest form of courage—moral courage. If you're having difficulty with your mental health, tell someone you trust. Support is closer than you think.

- Balancing the digital world and physical world is vital to your physical, mental, and spiritual fitness. People need friendship, connection, and authentic validation—needs that are not fully met by social media and technology. Disconnecting from the online world is one of the best ways to clear your head and improve your overall well-being.

- Taking a course, learning a language, painting/ creating art, or finding a hobby can strengthen your cognitive abilities.

- Understanding your emotions and practicing stress management can help you control your stress response and is just as important as stimulating the mind.

You may be surprised to learn that the mind doesn't require the same amount of attention as the body. The mind needs far more. So, we must work hard to build our mental toughness.

Spiritual Fitness

Living a balanced life isn't just about developing a healthy body and mind—it's also about growing spiritually. Spiritual fitness involves the values, beliefs, and faith that give life purpose and guide our every action. Although we each have our own convictions and traditions, we connect through our shared search for meaning, harmony, and belonging. This journey may involve regular meditation, prayer, affirmations, or any spiritual practice that connects us with something greater than ourselves, such as nature, community, or a higher power.

Achieving spiritual growth requires a level of vulnerability often discouraged by society but welcomed among certain tribes and social groups. Regardless of our individual beliefs, Everyday Warriors work together to make progress, encourage self-reflection, and foster acceptance within our hearts. Acceptance does not imply that you agree with another person's views, opinions, or beliefs; it simply means you respect their right to have them.

Spiritual fitness is different for each of us, but if it's an area that interests you, these ideas might help you get started:

- Give back through volunteerism, social contributions, community participation, and other acts of service.

- Learn to experience joy in watching others succeed; celebrating the success of others removes the need for comparison, which can deplete our spiritual fitness and lead to depression.

- Develop strong personal relationships. In this technology-obsessed world, people seem more connected to their screens than to each other—
all the more reason to invest in human interaction.

- Spend time in nature. Without a cell phone or internet connection, we naturally turn inward and reflect. When I'm in nature, I feel so small—but in the most amazing way. Recognizing my place in the vast natural world is an invitation to do more, to be more, and to treat others with respect and kindness. Even a thirty-minute walk at the end of the day can help build spiritual fitness.

- Let go of negativity and embrace optimism, forgiveness, and expressions of compassion. When we forgive, it helps relieve the negativity generated by painful memories and experiences.

There are countless other spiritual fitness goals to strive for, including practicing mindfulness, being fully present in everything we do, listening with our heart, leading through love, and recognizing opportunities for growth in each challenge we face.

One of my favorite quotes, commonly attributed to Alexander the Great, is "Bury my body and don't build any monument. Keep my hands out so the people know the one who won the world had nothing in hand when he died." We come into this world with nothing, and leave it the same way. Embrace the spiritual and shed the material. Consider this: who would you be if you had no house, no car, and no money? You'd be the true you. Nurturing that part of yourself is at the core of spiritual fitness.

LOSING AND REGAINING YOUR BALANCE

Balance is complex, and here's the truth: there's no such thing as being 100% balanced. Like perfection, it's an illusion that's impossible to achieve because life is constantly changing. That's why you must always be ready to pivot and readjust your priorities.

How do I know so much about balance? Unfortunately, it's because I know what losing it feels like. As part of a particularly specialized team of SEALs, I served alongside some of the highest-performing individuals in the world. I was in awe of the extraordinary balance some of them attained, not to mention their ability to sustain it through years of countless combat deployments. To perform at that level, I had to give it everything I had—which came at the expense of my balance. Nobody can keep up an unrelenting pace forever. Eventually, I hit a wall and entered the darkest period of my life, which ultimately ended my career in Special Operations. When I realized that my tank was empty, it forced the most difficult decision I'd ever made: to voluntarily leave my tribe, my support network, and the profession I loved and had spent my entire adult life building.

During more than ten combat deployments, fighting a determined and brutal enemy, I'd become so fixated on my leadership and tactical abilities that I'd allowed every other part of my life to experience atrophy. No longer being a military warrior meant I was losing my sense of purpose and identity. Although I was the most physically fit I'd ever been, it didn't matter, because I was mentally and spiritually bereft.

Soon, I began drinking heavily and became self-destructive. Instead of being vulnerable and letting someone know I was struggling, I pretended everything was fine. Everyone else saw me smiling and having fun, but deep down, I knew I was lost and in trouble.

For far too long, I had leaned on my military tribe and soaked in the sense of homecoming and belonging they provided. My military service fueled my spirit. While at war, I was spiritual in that I prayed for the well-being of those around me, but this type of spirituality was situational and transactional. So, after leaving the military, I reflected on who I was and what I believed. I worked on building up my mental and spiritual pillars so I could realign them with the physical pillar I'd hyper-focused on for so long. I've since regained some semblance of balance, which grows stronger each day. The progress I've made is thanks to the help of my new tribe, especially Dr. Chris Frueh, a psychologist who has helped me and many of my brothers-in-arms.

I'm not saying I've achieved complete balance (remember, it doesn't exist), but I am making progress one step ATTA time. That's all any of us can ever hope to do. You don't need perfect balance; you just need a little more than you had yesterday. By working on your physical, mental, and spiritual fitness, you are on the way to achieving the life you want and being your best self for those you care about.

After Action Review

- What parts of your life are currently out of balance? Why?

- Physical Fitness:

  * Rate your physical fitness on a 10-point scale (1 being extremely unfit and 10 being extremely fit).

* Identify three physical fitness goals and assign each a timeframe of 30, 60, or 90 days. (Write these target dates on your calendar.)

* List the top three things you'll do to make progress toward achieving these goals, starting *now*.

- Mental Fitness:

  * Rate your mental fitness on a 10-point scale (1 being extremely unfit and 10 being extremely fit).

  * Identify three mental fitness goals and assign each a timeframe of 30, 60, or 90 days. (Write these target dates on your calendar.)

  * List the top three things you'll do to make progress toward achieving these goals, starting *now*.

- Spiritual Fitness:

  * Rate your spiritual fitness on a 10-point scale (1 being extremely unfit and 10 being extremely fit).

* Identify three spiritual fitness goals and assign each a timeframe of 30, 60, or 90 days. (Write these target dates on your calendar.)

* List the top three things you'll do to make progress toward achieving these goals, starting *now*.

Key Takeaways

• The whole person concept is about focusing on the entirety of your health, including the three pillars of physical, mental, and spiritual fitness.

• Pursuing balance is essential because these three pillars exist in concert with one another. Only through the pursuit of balance can you reach your full potential.

• While we all lose our balance at some point, we all have the capacity to regain it.

4

IT BEGINS AND ENDS WITH YOU: KNOW THYSELF AND DEFINE THINE OWN SUCCESS

There's no tried-and-true path to how we achieve success.

—DR. JONNY KIM

DR. JONNY KIM IS ONE OF THE MOST ACCOMPLISHED INDIviduals in the world. We went through BUD/S together, and I had the privilege of serving alongside him on SEAL Team 3 during the Battle of Ramadi (2006) and the Battle of Sadr City (2008), for which he was awarded a Silver Star and Bronze Star, respectively. After two combat deployments, he earned a bachelor's degree in mathematics, graduating with a 3.98

GPA, followed by a doctorate of medicine from Harvard Medical School. Later, NASA selected him out of 18,000 applicants for their astronaut candidate program, which he completed in 2019. Even more impressive, Dr. Kim accomplished all of this by thirty-four years old.

Decorated Navy SEAL. Doctor of medicine. NASA astronaut. Dr. Kim is one of the most impressive people I've ever known, and I'm humbled to call him a brother-in-arms. While his level of success is extraordinary, he believes that others, especially his children, should not define their success based on his. "It's important to me that we all make our own mark in this world, and we make that mark the way we want to," he says.

So, what was the catalyst for such an enlightened perspective? Part of it was that his father's strict definition of success did not align with what he wanted out of life, a reality that caused many internal and external battles. "I don't think anyone should have to live in someone's shadow," he says. "Measuring ourselves against our parents or anyone is not the right way of thinking. I tell my children that I care not what they do—military, business, artist—my only request is that they are passionate and put their all into it."

UNDERSTANDING WHAT YOU WANT IN LIFE

Knowing where you are, who you are, and what you want is essential to living a purposeful and impactful life. Before executing a mission in the military, we'd receive a detailed explanation of the steps required to achieve the objective and a clear definition of success. It was called the "commander's intent," with a key component being the "desired end state."

Everyone should develop a commander's intent and desired end state, including you. Doing so can help you identify your objectives, outline the steps or milestones needed to achieve them, and establish a clear definition of success. Asking yourself what you want out of life can seem like a simple question, yet it's unassumingly complex. Many of us are so distracted by our everyday battles that we fail to realize we lack a clearly defined goal. If we continue living this toxic cycle, we might wake up one day to find we have never reached our full potential.

Knowing ourselves and what we want doesn't come easy because we face societal norms and expectations from the day we are born. For our entire lives, external influences, including family, teachers, and the media, have imposed their definition of success on us. Predictably, it's often narrow and hyper-focused on money, a prestigious career, and material possessions. But just because that idea of success is all around us, that doesn't mean we have to buy into it. The expectations of those around you can't control your mindset, what you focus on, or how your life turns out. Thankfully, those things are up to you and you alone.

Most of us are never encouraged to devote time to understanding ourselves through inward focus and reflection. These practices do not necessarily align with the values of our modern world. Today, society promotes seeking validation from everyone but ourselves. Countless daily distractions make it difficult to focus long enough to stop, think, and appreciate life. Social media has compounded this problem exponentially. There's no doubt that technology has increased our ability to communicate with people worldwide. Amazing as that may be, it's also become a measuring stick by which we obsessively compare ourselves to others. We set goals based on optics and the opinions of others rather than what we truly want. Even if we meet these goals, they're nothing more than empty wins. Unless you're an influencer, the numbers of followers and likes you accumulate have no real value. We can't say the same about the damage it's causing us physically, mentally, and spiritually—that couldn't be more real.

Suppose someone doesn't take the time to build self-awareness or develop a commander's intent rooted in introspection. They'll spend their entire life grinding without ever getting any closer to the life they truly want. Knowing thyself is a step many people skip when pursuing achievement, one with the potential of derailing everything. As an Everyday Warrior, you must develop the discipline to focus on your commander's intent, your definition of success or end state, and the mark you'd like to leave on the world. Start by taking an honest inventory of your capabilities, your goals, and the impact you want to have.

HOW DO YOU DEFINE SUCCESS?

The *Suda*, a tenth-century Byzantine encyclopedia, includes the aphorism *Nosce te ipsum*, which translates to "Know thyself." Success is accomplishing an aim or purpose, but nobody can tell you what that is, because you alone define your success. To help you decide what that is, ask yourself these questions:

- What do I want?

- What makes me happy?

- What's important to me, does it provide purpose and fulfillment, and does it directly or indirectly impact those around me?

When I define success in my life, I consider the pillars of physical, mental, and spiritual fitness. For me, balance is a crucial indicator of achievement. You may or may not want to consider these three pillars when defining your success; that is for you to decide. Navigating this process isn't easy, nor should it be. Identifying success is a long journey that can take many years (even decades) to figure out. Most likely, your definition of success will evolve with age and that's okay. What you value at forty-five may differ from what you valued at twenty-five. Only time will tell.

Conduct a Personal Inventory

One of the most critical pieces of information on the battle-field is the current location of your unit. Without knowing your coordinates, you can't navigate to the next destination. In other words—you're lost. You'd be surprised how many adults have little or no concept of where they're at in life. For most, spending time and energy focused on their strengths and weaknesses has never occurred to them. They've never thought about their attributes and characteristics, let alone inventoried them.

While knowing yourself includes understanding what you want to achieve in life, it's also taking a personal inventory, a self-assessment of your capabilities. This is a subjective and objective examination of your strengths and weaknesses. An honest assessment will help you identify strengths and areas that need improvement. Taking a personal inventory is about being realistic and candidly honest with yourself. We tend to resist situations that challenge us or make us feel uncomfort-able, but this only limits our potential and growth. Don't shy away from unpleasant truths.

If a teenage boy dreams of playing in the NBA but stops grow-ing at five feet, three inches tall, he needs to consider how that factors into his definition of success. This is not to say such a dream is impossible; Muggsy Bogues is that height and was arguably one of the greatest to play the game. Regardless of whether the boy dreaming of stardom makes it to the NBA, true success will be measured by the discipline, commitment, and resiliency he builds along the way, lessons that'll serve him well throughout his life regardless of where it leads.

Evaluating your strengths and weaknesses is not a one-and-done experience. Circumstances change, and you are constantly growing and learning. I may not know you personally, but I'm confident you're not the same person you were last year or even last month. Therefore, self-assessment must be a lifelong process. Start by periodically asking yourself these simple questions:

- What are my strongest attributes?

- What are my most critical areas of weakness?

- What have I learned, and am I satisfied with it?

- Do my strengths align with attributes needed to reach my goals?

- How can I push myself to continue learning and growing?

- What should I do differently to stay on track and achieve success?

Conducting this personal inventory at the beginning of each week works best for me; it gives me a framework and lets me know the areas to focus on throughout the next seven days. If weekly doesn't work for you, try monthly, or at the very least quarterly. Checking in with yourself at regular intervals allows you to adjust and reprioritize as needed. This will keep you on track toward your goals by making it possible to leverage your strengths while accounting for your weaknesses.

Collect Additional Data

Nobody knows you better than you know yourself, but you should not be the only source of information when conducting a personal inventory. Seeing ourselves clearly can be challenging; we might overlook a strength or have blind spots for a weakness that affects our ability to be objective. Asking those around you to honestly weigh in on your strengths and weaknesses (referred to as a *360 review* in the business world) will give you a far more accurate picture than you could ever build yourself. Their perspective and feedback will be a powerful tool on your journey.

For me, leaving the SEALs and beginning business endeavors required a lot of reflection. Although my background in Special Operations gave me invaluable skills, not all of these assets transfer to the business world. When I looked to my mentors for guidance, they helped me recognize that approaching the boardroom like a battlefield was not the best strategy. I needed to stop viewing everyone as an enemy or a potential threat. They coached me on the value of empathy and taught me the power of deliberate response rather than instant reaction.

In addition to relying on the perspectives of people you trust, you can use aptitude and personality tests as part of your self-assessment. Of course, these tools have varying accuracy and scientific relevance, so choose wisely and never give them too much weight. Align the information they provide with what you already know and decide how the additional data can benefit your growth goals.

Focus on Impact

Money isn't the most significant currency in life; impact is. You can't appraise the value of making a difference in someone's life. In this way, Warren Buffett is no more successful than a teacher or a coach (maybe even less so). Don't get me wrong, earning money is not evil, but it also won't comfort you in your final days. Do you know what will? The people you've helped. I've met wealthy people who were rich in the bank but poor in character, and people struggling to pay rent whose impact on the world made them far richer than the 1%.

Everyone's definition of success is uniquely their own, but impact is a crucial component regardless of who you are or what you want to achieve. As a social species, humans base much of our self-worth on how we impact others. We do this because it brings us fulfillment, purpose, and joy. Leading a fulfilling life means impacting your family, friends, community, and the world around you. You could be a CEO who mentors employees, a leader who sets an example by acting with integrity, or a proud mother or father who never misses your child's games. Regardless of who you are or how much is in your bank account, you can still make an impact.

We can't help but have an impact on others, so why not act with intention? Our impact happens over time and is like an apple seed; we plant it today, water it tomorrow, and take comfort in knowing its fruit will be enjoyed long after we're gone. Think about what's important to you and what you want your legacy to be. It doesn't need to be something big because even small acts of kindness have a ripple effect.

In 2014, Admiral William H. McRaven addressed the graduating class at the University of Texas. During his commencement speech, he explained, "If every one of you changed the lives of just ten people, and each one of those folks changed the lives of another ten people...then, in five generations...you will have changed the lives of 800 million people." Consider that when planting your apple seed.

THE POWER OF IMPACT:
A LETTER FROM JIMMY

Retiring from the military sent me spiraling down and led to destructive, self-loathing habits. Leaving such a tight-knit community meant I wasn't only losing a job but also losing my sense of purpose and identity. I was lost professionally and personally. In 2017, when I was at my lowest point, I received an email from Jimmy, a young Marine who'd served under me in a combat zone three years earlier.

* * *

Sir,

I hope this is your email. I served under you as 1st Lieutenant in 2014. You plucked me from a benign assignment as a Marine LNO, made me your operations officer, and taught me more about being an officer and a leader in three months than I could appreciate at the time.

Right before we left for the outpost, you gave me an American flag patch off of your sleeve so that I would match the rest of the SEAL Troop. Last week I wore that patch on my body armor when I was asked to lead an entry team serving a warrant in the Bronx, my first since leaving the Marines and taking a federal law enforcement position. The team was inexperienced, so I started with a ROC (Rehearsal of Concept) drill, progressed to rehearsals, and finished with smooth execution; except for the fact that our target wasn't there. Nonetheless, my superiors were impressed with the execution. As I unpacked my gear that night and looked at that patch, I thought about how far I'd come since you handed it to me.

That American flag patch was on my shoulder on September 1st 2014 when the CH-53 I was riding in crashed into the ocean. I had to drop most of my personal equipment to make it out of the helo and up to the surface. I lost all the contact info I had written down, the SEAL Team coin, and most of the other little mementos from my time in your unit, but that American flag patch stayed with me.

After that first tour I became more serious about planning and preparing for operations, trading in my easygoing comedic ways for a more direct and task-oriented approach. Using methods which I had picked up from you and the guys on how to navigate the joint world, make liaison, and bring operational elements together, I was able to run circles around my peers during following assignments. I became my command's go-to man for complicated missions, leading several long-range operations into some less-than-reputable places.

I left the Marines a few months ago after being selected for a career-level education program that was going to take me out of the operating forces for so long that I'd be a dedicated staff officer by the time I got back. I'm still an active reservist and will probably be deploying again as soon as I can get myself attached to a deploying unit.

In summary, I want to thank you for the time you invested in me. I know there were occasions when I didn't have my act together, but you effectively fixed me. No superior officer I had ever had before or since truly took the time to mentor and develop subordinates the way you did. I made it a point to run small roundtable PME talks with my lieutenants much like you did for Jeff, Joe, and me. I'll take those lessons with me everywhere I serve. If there is anything I can do to help with you and your family, please don't hesitate to contact me.

* * *

I broke down in tears when I read that email. In 2014, I took Jimmy under my wing because I wanted him to develop into a better officer than I was, just as my mentors had done for me. In his email, he thanked me for the impact I'd made on him, but ironically, his impact on me far exceeded anything I could have ever done for him. Not only that, but he was reaching out when I needed it most. I was mentally and spiritually depleted, and his words became the fuel I needed to turn my life around. I am forever indebted to Jimmy for the impact he had on my life. Whether we realize it or not, we're all making an impact on someone—and it's powerful. Powerful enough that a simple email can pull a person from the darkness into the light. Powerful enough to save a life.

I have been trying to contact Jimmy for years, with no success. So if he is reading this: Thank you, brother. I love you and cannot thank you enough for lifting me up when I needed it most.

After Action Review

- Have others placed standards of success on you? What are those standards and who placed them?

- Are there facets of your life that you need to regain control of?

- What is *your* definition of success? Write out your commander's intent and desired end state. If you need help, consider the questions included earlier in the chapter:

* What do I want?

* What makes me happy?

* What's important to me, does it provide purpose and fulfillment, and does it directly or indirectly impact those around me?

Challenge: Remember to take a personal inventory every few months to reevaluate your strengths, areas for growth and improvement, and where you are in life.

Key Takeaways

• Success looks different for everyone. Strive for what *you* want—not what others think you should want.

• To get where you want to go, you must understand where you are. Regular self-assessments will help you better understand your strengths, weaknesses, and how to continue growing.

• Impact is the greatest currency in life. A life of impact is a life well lived.

5

FIGHTING THE EPIDEMIC OF VICTIMHOOD

Let me tell you something you already know. The world ain't all sunshine and rainbows. It's a very mean and nasty place, and I don't care how tough you are, it will beat you to your knees and keep you there permanently if you let it. You, me, or nobody is gonna hit as hard as life. But it ain't about how hard ya hit. It's about how hard you can get hit and keep moving forward. How much you can take and keep moving forward. That's how winning is done!

—SYLVESTER STALLONE, Rocky Balboa

IN 2010, MARINE ROB JONES LOST BOTH LEGS TO AN IMPRO-vised explosive device (IED) while serving in Afghanistan. Having experienced such a traumatic, life-altering injury, he could have easily chosen to relegate himself to victimhood—but he didn't. Nothing could stop Rob from embracing life and the challenges it brought his way.

Of course Rob experienced doubts, was overwhelmed with negativity, and likely even wanted to give up—as anybody in his situation would. But Rob refused to let losing his legs define him. What he did next not only defined him but it inspired millions.

After working through a long, painful, and frustrating recovery, Rob focused on raising money for veterans, including by completing thirty-one marathons in thirty-one days. That's right: thirty-one marathons in thirty-one days. He accepted the challenge of his injury, took control, and displayed a master class in determination.

We have a saying in the military: "The enemy gets a vote." In other words, you can plan and prepare all you want, but you can't control what others do or what life throws at you. Rob didn't choose to lose his legs, the enemy made that choice for him, but Rob was responsible for everything that followed.

Just as the enemy always gets a vote, so does life. The world will throw obstacles at you when you least expect it. When that happens, you have two choices: become the story's hero or its victim. You can't control everything, but you can control your attitude, mindset, and how you react to adversity.

THE DANGEROUS RISE
OF VICTIMHOOD

Victimhood runs rampant, especially here in the United States. Compared to much of the world, Americans enjoy an exceptionally high standard of living—one they've done nothing to earn. Because of this, instead of appreciation, many feel entitled. How can I say that without fearing repercussions? Because I've spent my career in war-torn, third-world countries and understand how much we take for granted.

The result of entitlement is a self-absorbed populace that lacks perspective and obsesses over what others have, which causes jealousy, envy, and animosity. Messaging around us further promotes the false belief that someone having more comes at the expense of others having less. So instead of working hard to achieve our goals, we blame other people, groups, institutions, and systems for our problems.

Unfortunately, victimhood is everywhere these days and is spreading like a virus. Victims wallow in negativity and bring others down with them. They look for validation in rejecting ownership of their lives. You've heard the saying: misery loves company. As humans, we naturally seek attention; embracing the victim mindset is an effective way of getting it because sharing our misfortunes often causes others to show empathy and sympathy. That attention leads to a self-perpetuating cycle that reinforces the idea that someone is indeed a victim and not to blame for their actions and choices.

Social media plays a prominent role in the victimhood epidemic. Numerous peer-reviewed studies have shown a connection between social media consumption and increased health risks, including depression, anxiety, loneliness, self-harm, and suicidal ideations. Incredibly, an entire subset of psychology has emerged due to this relatively young technology, which has only achieved mass adoption in the last fifteen years. Imagine what future data will show us about the potential psychological impact of social media on our cognitive development.

A quick look at the terms entering our social lexicon will show you that we're headed in a dangerous direction of victimhood:

- **Doomscrolling:** endlessly scrolling through negative and disheartening content, even when doing so makes us feel sad, overwhelmed, and hopeless.

- **Social media envy:** the feelings of inadequacy, jealousy, and envy that arise from browsing pictures and posts on social media.

- **FOMO (fear of missing out):** the fear of missing out after seeing others post about an event or experience on social media. This can lead to anxiety and other negative feelings.

Social media is not a reflection of reality. People only post a small snapshot of their lives—the curated highlights they want you to see. While most people are quick to share their accomplishments, very few are willing to share their struggles and failures. So, if our feeds are full of everyone else living extraordinary lives—without detail or context—it's only natural to feel like we're lacking. These misrepresentations of reality can negatively affect how we see our own life. Despite what other people appear to have, it's essential to recognize that no amount of followers or likes can insulate someone from adversity. Experiencing pain and hardship is simply part of life.

Social media also has a tendency to polarize and divide us. The internet is loaded with keyboard cowards who seem to derive twisted pleasure from antagonizing, demeaning, and bullying others. They do so while enjoying relative anonymity. I have no respect for trolls who baselessly instigate arguments, sow division, and attack people's character. While they may not receive consequences for their behavior, anyone who acts this way is already paying the price through their lack of purpose and self-respect. Hopefully, they realize their potential and do the introspective work necessary to become a force for good instead of remaining stagnant in their misery and self-loathing.

Everyone around us seems constantly poised for an argument. Even our elected officials—those entrusted with the solemn duty of leading our Constitutional Republic—often attack each other with blind hatred. They intentionally stoke the flames of unrest instead of setting an example of civil discourse between political parties with opposing governing philosophies.

Regardless, your battles are likely not external, but internal. Although those trying to sow division tell you differently, your struggles are rarely *you-versus-them* and far more likely to be *you-versus-you*. You are and always have been your worst enemy, not *them*. While keyboard cowards focus on hurting others, true warriors concentrate on bettering themselves and helping those around them.

Being a victim is easy since blaming others requires little effort; it's an excuse to avoid responsibility. Claiming victimhood whenever something goes wrong discounts our agency and removes us from the equation of our destiny. Forfeiting our sovereignty leads us down a dark path that runs in the opposite direction of our goals and dreams.

VICTIMHOOD IS A MINDSET

People often push back against the idea that we control most of what happens in our life—but that doesn't make it any less accurate.

In 2020, I was giving a virtual speech about taking ownership of your life when an audience member asked, "What about COVID? I won't take ownership of COVID." I explained that I didn't expect him to, but that he should take ownership of his response to the adversity and uncertainty posed by the pandemic.

Despite popular belief, life's not fair and it's not supposed to be. Most of us first hear this misguided concept around five years old; that's not a surprise since children are innocent and have a basic understanding of the world. It's another thing to have this misconception at fifty years old. Of course bad things happen that you can't control. That's not what makes you a victim. Your choice to be a victim or a warrior has nothing to do with external events and everything to do with your mindset. When life throws a curveball—like an illness or job loss—that's when your warrior mindset is an invaluable asset. It helps you adapt by formulating your next move and overcoming obstacles.

A person with a victim mindset believes they have no control over what happens to them. So they don't take responsibility, immediately quit when challenges arise, and give up all hope of success. Because they are never at fault, they always need someone to blame, creating a dangerous and volatile social dynamic.

Warriors, however, welcome challenges. Adversity comes with an opportunity to learn and grow. A warrior mindset allows us to take responsibility for our problems, pride in the solutions, and ownership of all outcomes. While it won't protect us from experiencing hardship, it does prepare us to respond in a healthy, productive way.

While there are some things in life that we can't plan for, let alone control, we certainly have control over our reactions to them. We all experience varying degrees of hardship, and the one thing we must never do is discount our own role in them. When good things happen to other people, we often say it was luck—but it's not that simple. Luck is often nothing more than being prepared when an opportunity presents itself. I could meet a record executive, but I wouldn't get a record deal unless I had spent years practicing and training. If I had, would that be luck or hard work and determination paying off? In the end, *fortune favors the prepared.*

To shift our mindset from victim to warrior, we must remember that we're in control of our life by starting the day in the right frame of mind. For me, it means waking up each morning and sitting on the edge of my bed, rotating my feet (a necessity due to nerve damage caused by grenade shrapnel and as a reminder to be grateful that I'm still here), and saying, "Today's going to be harder, but that's what I'm here for." Then, leaving my phone in airplane mode, I step into my home gym, "The Small Minds Repair Shop," and prepare myself mentally and physically for the day ahead.

Only you can decide how you'll approach life's battles. It starts by taking ownership of your choices and your response to challenges.

THE SCARY REALITY OF
SOCIAL MEDIA USE

The average person spends 2.5 hours on social media each day. Take that and extrapolate it over time, and it gets even scarier.

- Every day = 2.5 hours

- Every week = 17.5 hours

- Every month = 75 hours (nearly two workweeks)

- Every year = 912 hours (38 days)

- By age 50 = 1,400 days (3.85 years)**

- By age 70 = 2,100 days (5.75 years)**

**Assuming social media consumption starting at age twelve.

This is great for marketers, advertisers, and data miners but horrible for us. This is time that you could use to pursue your goals, foster genuine relationships, or engage in self-care.

SHIFT HOW YOU USE SOCIAL MEDIA

How you use social media has a significant impact on your mindset. At its best, social media leads to unlikely friendships, powers positive social movements, and helps family and friends remain active in each other's lives regardless of distance. At its worst, social media amplifies the darker side of human nature—including hatred, jealousy, and spite. Social media is not inherently evil, but it's difficult to experience the good side without also being exposed to the bad.

In "No More FOMO: Limiting Social Media Decreases Loneliness and Depression," researchers from the University of Pennsylvania identified a causal link between decreased social media use and a reduction in depression and loneliness. They also found that just the act of self-monitoring usage can decrease anxiety. So rather than give social media up altogether, we can rethink how we use it.

First, pay attention to the content you're consuming. Like everything in life, positivity breeds positivity, and negativity breeds negativity. Asking yourself these three simple questions will help you determine if your social media use could be promoting a victimhood mindset. Does your time on social media:

1. Make you feel like you're owed something?

2. Make you feel bad or angry about who you are, what you have, or how you look?

3. Make you jealous of those who appear to have more (fun, money, attention, etc.) than you do?

Second, adopt the motto *Don't compare, but be aware.* Unfortunately, in today's hyperconnected world, life is often treated as a competition. Life isn't about winning or losing; it's about experiencing joy and being present in the moment. The comparisons social media encourages are harmful to our physical, mental, and spiritual well-being. While others' achievements can be used as motivation, comparing yourself will not help you attain your goals.

Finally, take the opportunity to be a creator, not just a follower. Use social media to tell your own story, but instead of being part of the problem, be a part of the solution by sharing your failures as often as your successes. This allows those watching to see your progress, which is much healthier than just showing off your victories without providing context. Seeking guidance from those around you and sharing encouragement with others will help you retain a positive mindset.

FREEING YOURSELF FROM THE VICTIMHOOD MINDSET

Nobody ever sets out with the intention of letting the victim mindset take hold in their life. Still, it happens. The most effective tool to fight it is acknowledging it exists and understanding what triggers it. Consider these common causes and the strategies to combat them:

- **You like things to come easy:** Easy has become the default mode for a lot of people. But things worth having rarely come easy. If you want something to change, you need to work hard. As the saying goes, "If it were easy, everyone would do it."

- **You've experienced loss or hardship:** When something terrible happens that's out of your control, feeling angry is a normal, healthy response. It's part of the healing process. Use your feelings as fuel. Give yourself time to reflect and then focus on taking action.

- **You're jealous of others:** Remember, comparison is the thief of joy. One of the best ways to combat envy is to cultivate gratitude. Appreciate what you have instead of worrying about what you don't. Take a few minutes each day to write down a few things you're grateful for. Additionally, go out of your way to find happiness in other people's joy and accomplishments. Nothing brings me more fulfillment than watching my teammates and friends succeed.

- **You feel overwhelmed and powerless:** When things feel out of your control, select one small action and focus on that. Small tasks are accomplishments too, and enough small victories eventually make a big difference. "One step ATTA time" is my daily reminder on how to live life. It applies to almost everything. One meal ATTA time. One workout ATTA time. One relationship ATTA time. (More on this in Chapter 7, "One Step ATTA Time.")

- **You want attention:** We all crave connection and validation from those around us, but there are positive and negative ways of getting it. Consider healthy, constructive ways to garner attention; it can be as simple as telling a friend you need to talk.

- **You're surrounded by people with a victim mindset:** I'll get into this more in Chapter 10, "We All Need a Tribe," but the people around you—your tribe—are critical to your mindset and integral to your success. They can also instigate your downfall if you let them. Be thoughtful about who you spend time with, including on social media. If necessary, remove negative influences from your life.

To live a positive, healthy, and productive life, you've got to expunge victimhood from it. There's a gap between where you are and where you want to be. To close that gap and achieve your goals, you must take ownership. Only then can you start taking steps to control your outcomes. Understand that no matter what the obstacle is, you have a choice. It may not be a choice that determines the final result, but you always have a choice in how you handle the situation.

After Action Review

Let's face it, eliminating social media entirely is unrealistic, but if you want to achieve your goals, limiting the time you spend online is crucial. The journey toward success will require you to step away from the screen and engage in the physical world. The aforementioned University of Pennsylvania study found that restricting social media use to thirty minutes a day resulted in a significant reduction in anxiety, depression, loneliness, sleep problems, and FOMO.

I recommend trying these social media challenges to ease into the transition. Here's something to remember: give yourself room to fail. If you slip up, just recommit, refocus, and push forward.

- **Unplug on Friday:** Commit to logging off social media Friday evening through Sunday evening. If that's too much, start with Saturday and build from there. Spend this time with family and friends, free from distraction. Go live your own adventure. Even if you record it, wait until Monday to post it.

- **Set limits:** Limit your social media use to two daily thirty-minute sessions. This will help prevent you from mindlessly swiping when you're bored. Even though you may go through social media withdrawal, I assure you, you're not missing anything.

- **Stick to the basics:** Use your phone for the bare essentials during the workday. That means phone calls and texting. When we rely too much on our smartphones, it's all too easy to go from checking emails to watching videos on our social feeds.

- **Eliminate the bell:** Get in the habit of putting your phone in airplane mode while working, so you're not distracted by notifications. Much like behavioral conditioning trained Pavlov's dog to salivate at the sound of a bell, we crave a burst of dopamine each time our phone dings.

Pro tip: Find an accountability partner, preferably someone who's close by, to keep you on track.

Key Takeaways

- When we give in to the victimhood mindset, we relinquish our power and stop moving forward.

- While things will happen that you can't control, how you handle them is something you can.

- Don't blame the success of others for what you don't have. Remember that what we see of others' accomplishments is only a fraction of their story. Success requires hard work and failure.

- Social media can add value to our lives, but it can also lead to an influx of comparison and negativity. Be aware of your online activities and keep a rein on your social media consumption.

6

DOING > TALKING: SET AN INTENTION, PLAN, ACT, REFLECT, REPEAT

If you talk about it, it's a dream; if you envision it, it's possible; but if you schedule it, it's real.

—TONY ROBBINS

BOBBY ESTELL WAS BORN IN HOT SPRINGS, ARKANSAS, TO teenage parents—his mother was fifteen and his father seventeen. It wasn't long before his father left. Living in poverty, his mother turned to her family for help. They packed their few possessions and moved to the small town of Mountain Pine; while they were still struggling, at least his maternal grandmother could help raise him. Times were hard, but Bobby always believed that radio was his way to a better life. At seventeen years old, he took a significant step toward realizing his dream when he landed a job at KSWH-FM, the campus radio station at Henderson State University. During his time at the station, the on-air personality of Bobby Bones was born.

Five years later, Bobby graduated from Henderson with a BA in communication and accepted a job at Q100/KQAR in Little Rock, Arkansas. He soon found that he was considered atypical by industry standards. In fact, the *Washington Post* wrote that he lacked the "classic, booming radio DJ voice." But Bones knew what he was meant to do and had a plan to achieve his goals. So, he blocked out the noise and focused on perfecting his craft through hard work, practice, and reflection.

Despite the negative feedback, Bones was offered his own show on Austin's KHFI-FM. Over the next ten years, he worked tirelessly to grow his audience and build his tribe, resulting in *The Bobby Bones Show* becoming Austin's highest-ranked morning radio show. Recognizing that they had a valuable commodity, iHeartMedia moved the show to Nashville and launched it into national syndication. Their investment in Bobby paid dividends as the show quickly became one of the most popular nationally syndicated shows in the United States.

After achieving his original goal, Bobby expanded his dreams. While he may have been most comfortable behind the microphone, his appearances on ABC's *Dancing with the Stars* and *American Idol* made it clear that he had crossover appeal.

Having conquered two mediums, Bones turned his attention to publishing, where he found success with two *New York Times* best sellers. His latest book, *Fail Until You Don't: Fight, Grind, Repeat,* is a manual for those looking to achieve success on their own terms. While there are many lessons we can take from Bobby's story, the most important is that it doesn't matter who you are, where you're from, or what others say—all that matters is your determination to set intentions, act, reflect, and repeat. That's why Bobby Bones is an excellent example of what it means to be an Everyday Warrior.

HUMANS ARE *REALLY* BAD AT FOLLOWING THROUGH

Goals are easy to dream but hard to achieve. That's because very few people are willing to do what it takes. By now, you've heard all the cliches:

- Talk is cheap.

- Actions speak louder than words.

- I don't trust words; I trust actions.

- Actions always prove why words mean nothing.

While tiresome, there's a reason these sayings are overused: they're all true.

I'd never discourage anyone from dreaming big. We should all dare greatly. But setting a goal is only a tiny part of the success equation. Putting in the work is far more important. Spend time in the Special Operations community and you'll hear the phrase "doing is greater than talking." The shorthand form of this is: Doing > Talking.

Saying we're going to do something is completely different than doing it. That is why 80% of New Year's resolutions are abandoned within the first forty-five days. There's more than enough empirical data showing humans are bad at following through. This happens for many reasons.

Not Enough Time

Life pulls us in many different directions—family, work, self-care, and social obligations. Being surrounded by distractions makes getting things done even more challenging. Soon, we start to believe there's not enough time in the day and feel overwhelmed. If we think of time as scarce, our goals will always be just out of reach. The truth is, we have enough time—but lack the discipline to use it efficiently. Each day is 1,440 minutes long, and the average person spends 150 minutes of it on social media. Reallocating those 2.5 hours to achieving our goals leaves us with 1,290 minutes. Once again, time is not in short supply—but our ability to prioritize it is.

Not Wanting to Put in the Work

Nothing in life is free—that goes double for success. Maintaining the momentum, focus, and discipline needed to achieve our goals is hard. But anything worth having is worth earning. Accomplishing what matters most requires that we sacrifice less meaningful pursuits. Those in business will recognize this concept as opportunity cost, giving up the potential benefit of one action when choosing another. Taking a risk can be intimidating, but not taking it is far worse because there's no chance of success.

In this hyperconnected world, social media has given everybody a megaphone. With a few keystrokes, you can share your goals and bask in praise for simply stating an intention without doing any work. The validation once reserved for those who've overcome obstacles and achieved goals has lost value because we can get the same recognition for simply typing and hitting enter—but that's short-lived and empty. Feelings that accompany unearned validation evaporate, but the fulfillment of achieving your goals lasts forever.

Doubt and Fear

Nothing kills goals like doubt and fear. This duo will not only attempt to make you quit before you even start, but it'll always be there waiting for a moment of weakness to creep in. We doubt our abilities and fear the unknown, failure, and what others might think. I'll explain how to handle doubt and fear in Chapter 8, "Get Comfortable with Being Uncomfortable." For now, understand that achieving your goals takes courage. As Mark Twain said, "Courage is resistance to fear, mastery of fear—not absence of fear." Despite your fears, you must act.

Basically, it all comes down to the fact that talk is easy and action isn't. Talking about your goals won't change your life; making real progress requires syncing words and actions.

WHAT'S YOUR ROADBLOCK?

You may hit different roadblocks while working toward your goals. What's the solution? Well, that depends on the problem you're facing. Here are some solutions to common problems:

- **You're unwilling to put in the hard work:** It's called hard work for a reason—it's HARD! When the honeymoon phase wears off, the reality of just how much work you have sets in. One way to break through this roadblock is to evaluate your commitment early on. Many people set goals they don't care about and quit at the slightest sign of adversity. Your success relies on commitment, and only you know how committed you are.

- **You feel overwhelmed:** People become overwhelmed for many reasons, the primary being their goal is simply *too big* or *too vague*. Setting a significant goal can be both motivating and rewarding, but remember to be pragmatic. Set goals that are challenging but realistic, with a focus on clear, specific, achievable steps.

- **You don't believe in yourself:** Self-doubt and questioning your ability to achieve your goal before you even start will sideline you from ever achieving it. When setting a goal, you must believe in your ability to achieve it. Setting pragmatic goals will help, but to further build confidence, recall prior victories. They don't necessarily have to be related to your current goal. Just think about times when you put in hard work and overcame challenges.

- **You give up after failure:** Failing is hard—arguably one of the hardest things we ever have to overcome. When you hit the failure roadblock (which you will, because we all do), view it as just another step in your journey toward success. In the process of inventing the incandescent light bulb, Thomas Edison famously said, "I have not failed. I've just found 10,000 ways that won't work." Failing is a natural part of the process; approach new goals expecting setbacks. Preparing for failure now will help you overcome pitfalls later.

- **You make excuses:** Making excuses to avoid taking responsibility for our actions has become a habit for many of us. We may not even realize we're doing it. When something feels hard, the tendency toward a victim mindset shows up, and we start thinking:

  * *"I don't have time."* Then make it a priority.

  * *"I don't have the money."* We always find a way if something truly matters. If you don't have the money, borrow it, earn it, or secure sponsorships.

  * *"Now is not a good time."* There's no such thing as a good time...there's only right now.

  * *"Nobody will give me a chance."* You have to give yourself a chance before anybody else will.

* *"I'm too young, old, or ____."* Millions of people refuse to let age or any other barrier stop them. At sixteen years old, Malala Yousafzai was nominated for the Nobel Peace Prize after being shot in the head while advocating for women's rights. One-hundred-year-old Teiichi Igarashi reached Mt. Fuji's summit after making the 12,385-foot climb in his socks.

Stop finding reasons to quit. Instead, avoid excuses, set goals, make plans, and take action.

THE POWER OF ACTION: WHY YOUR WORDS AND ACTIONS MUST ALIGN

Without action, goals are just fleeting daydreams. You'll never be able to achieve the things you want. But there's another reason it's important for your words and actions to align: nothing erodes a person's reputation and credibility faster than being known as a big talker who can't back it up. Where I live in Texas, that's known as being "all hat, no cattle." Character is the most valuable asset any of us will ever have, but if we fail to follow through, that asset will quickly become an ever-growing expense. The lack of trust this creates will damage not only your relationships with other people, but also your relationship with yourself.

Following through is rarely the path of least resistance, especially when it comes to our ambitions and desires. I like to underpromise with my words and overdeliver through my actions—it's a win-win. That's one reason my business goals center on providing clients with more value than I take, a philosophy I work hard to follow in all aspects of my life.

Each of us has an incredible power that we must learn to embrace; it's the power of action. When you say you're going to do something, deliver—even if it causes you hardship. The most significant accolade in Special Operations, or any profession, is being called dependable and reliable. We can depend on reliable people and rely on dependable people. Dependable people are trustworthy and give their all to achieve an objective, no matter the circumstances. Reliable people consistently demonstrate a solid work ethic and always come through when they're needed most.

How can you ensure that your words and actions align? It all comes down to setting a goal and creating a plan.

FRAMEWORK FOR SUCCESS

Guess what happens to lofty goals when there's no plan—they evaporate.

Maybe this year, you want to lose thirty pounds or save $15,000. Those are great goals, but accomplishing them without knowing your objective and setting measurable steps will be nearly impossible. Without a process or framework to gauge and evaluate your success, you're like a rudderless ship at sea, floating in no particular direction.

Achieving your goals will be challenging, but that doesn't mean it's impossible. It just means it's worth working for. Remember how old video game systems had secret codes? You'd press up, down, A, B, left, right and get unlimited lives. Well, there's something like that for aligning your words and actions. Instead of entering a secret code, you follow five simple steps. The best part is that finishing the level is way more fulfilling in real life.

#1: Set an Intention

Your intention is your goal, but did you know that not all goals are created equal? It's true. SMART goals are objectively better and more likely to be successful. *SMART* is an acronym for Specific, Measurable, Attainable, Relevant, and Time-based.

- **Specific:** It's essential to define your goals with focus and specificity. Decide what success means to you—two people can have the same goal but very different definitions of success. If you want to get in shape, that can mean you want to lose weight, build lean muscle, or increase endurance. Instead, be more specific by saying you want to lose fifteen pounds, gain five pounds of muscle, or run a half marathon in a specific amount of time. This level of exactness will give you a clear objective.

- **Measurable:** You've set a specific goal; now, make sure you can measure your progress. Figure out how to quantify your hard work. How else will you know when you hit milestones or achieve your goal? Objective measurements provide the data needed to make corrections and ensure you're moving in the right direction.

- **Attainable:** Consider whether your goal is realistic. While losing five pounds is realistic, breaking Tom Brady's Super Bowl record is most likely not (at least for 99.999% of Americans). Select a goal that stretches your abilities while remaining achievable. If you make it too easy, you're not challenging yourself. If you make it too hard, you're setting yourself up for failure. Whatever you choose, make sure to give it time.

- **Relevant:** Think about why you want to achieve each of your goals. Reach an understanding of why these goals are relevant to you. Consider how these goals will impact your life. But make sure you are focused on you. Forget about what other people want. This is all about what you want to achieve. Reflecting on how these goals connect with what you want out of life will keep you motivated.

- **Time-Based:** Set a clear and reasonable time-frame for your goal. Not having enough time will cause stress and anxiety, but having too much time could lead to procrastination and loss of focus. When we set a deadline, there's a tendency for the work to expand to fill that time. If you give yourself a week to complete a two-hour task, the task will take you all week to complete. An accurate timeline keeps you focused and motivated and makes establishing milestones and small victories easier.

#2: Make a Plan

Before you can act, you must map out the specific, actionable steps needed to achieve your goal. In other words, make a plan. Just because you're active doesn't mean you're achieving. A solid plan helps you avoid this trap by laying out the steps and milestones essential to your success.

A goal may take months or even years to achieve. It can be challenging to focus on progress when success seems so far in the future. A simple solution that makes even the most ambitious goals manageable is breaking each goal into smaller, more manageable tasks—called *chunking*. Achieving these small victories will empower you, keep you motivated, and make your progress clear.

Another strategy is *reverse planning*, where you start with the end goal and work backward. Here's an example. I want to lose thirty pounds in the next eight months; therefore, I must lose one pound each week (that's SMART). I've built in a two-week cushion to allow for adjustments. At the end of each week, I will conduct weigh-ins. The data from these milestones will help determine the need to adjust my workouts and diet depending on if I'm ahead or behind schedule. (We will discuss both chunking and reverse planning in more detail in the next chapter, "One Step ATTA Time.")

#3: Take Action

You've set an intention and developed a plan. What's next? The time for talking is over—it's time to take action. While this is exciting, it's also the most challenging step in the entire process. Still, you've got this.

Taking action requires two things: time and effort. Any time you pursue a new goal, you have to assess your priorities and reallocate your time accordingly. Thankfully, all the work you've done getting to know yourself and defining your success is about to pay off. You may start worrying about missing your usual activities—this is natural. Focusing on your progress will help you see that those activities you miss now will never bring you closer to your goals. Often, people find that relying on those familiar routines and comfortable habits is what held them back for so long.

Soon you'll realize that your greatest asset is self-discipline. We don't achieve goals through short bursts of frantic activity but through steady, consistent effort. That constant effort requires discipline. Don't worry if you don't consider yourself a disciplined person; Chapter 9, "The Warrior Way," will help you build self-discipline, self-accountability, and positive habits.

#4: Take Time to Reflect

Taking the time for introspective reflection teaches us lessons and helps us pinpoint necessary adjustments that keep us on track. Although it's an essential part of the framework, we often assume reflection happens naturally, but it doesn't. We must build reflection into the process with intention.

Additionally, reflection should not be an afterthought triggered once we achieve our goal. We should incorporate it throughout the entire process to stay focused, recognize progress and challenges, and make necessary adjustments. You will fall short of meeting some of your milestones and benchmarks along the way. It helps to know that it's simply part of achieving success. Reflection is the tool that lets you reassess, adapt, and overcome when it happens.

When reflecting, these four simple questions will help you assess your progress and implement changes. Ask yourself:

1. Where am I now, and how does that compare to where I planned to be?

2. What did I plan to happen, and what actually happened?

3. What steps can I take to get back on track?

4. What changes can I implement to be more effective and efficient?

#5: Repeat

After the final step, you complete the cycle and return to the beginning. None of us will ever reach a point where we know everything; there will always be new goals and challenges to conquer. Each time you restart the process, you'll be more accomplished and capable. Get back in the arena and prepare for your next battle!

After Action Review

Identify a goal, and now make it SMART:

Example: Lose thirty pounds in four months to look and feel healthier. That's specific (thirty pounds), measurable (you can weigh yourself), attainable (you have to lose under two pounds a week), relevant (it will improve your life), and time-based (four months).

Specific:

Measurable:

Attainable:

Relevant:

Time-based:

Key Takeaways

- When working toward a goal, actions will always trump words, but the actions need to be intentional and focused.

- Roadblocks and challenges are an inevitable part of any path to success. Be prepared for them and use them as fuel to keep you focused and moving forward.

- Embrace the five-step framework—set an intention, make a plan, take action, reflect, and repeat—trust yourself to do the work.

7

ONE STEP ATTA TIME: SUCCESS ISN'T BOUGHT, IT'S EARNED

Every step you take has brought you to where you are today. Looking back...I realize that all [of my] little successes have added up to all the big ones. There is no failure because...every step leads you and teaches you.

—NIMSDAI PURJA, former UK Special Boat Service Operator, author of Beyond Possible, and star of the Netflix documentary *14 Peaks: Nothing Is Impossible*

HAVE YOU EVER MET SOMEONE WHO KNEW EXACTLY WHAT they were meant to do from a very young age? If so, you know how remarkable it is. At eight years old, Bethany Hamilton knew she wanted to be a professional surfer and understood better than most that her journey mattered. Instead of playing with toys, like other kids her age, she spent her free time perfecting her technique, sharpening her skills, and waxing her board.

After four years of practice, she was more passionate than ever—but then her life changed. On Friday, October 31, 2003, the thirteen-year-old planned on spending Halloween surfing with friends; this wasn't anything special since this is how she spent most days. After catching a few decent waves, she took a moment to float on her board and enjoy the clean breeze. Without warning, a fourteen-foot tiger shark severed Bethany's arm just below the shoulder. Suffering such a horrific attack is enough to scare anybody away from the ocean, but not Bethany.

Less than a month later, she was back on her surfboard. Over the next three years, she made the necessary adjustments and only got better. At sixteen years old, Bethany turned pro, and she is now one of the best surfers in the world. While she knew her journey was essential to making her who she needed to be, her drive, determination, and spirit are what set her apart from the competition.

IT'S ABOUT THE JOURNEY, NOT THE DESTINATION

Life is a long journey. So, it stands to reason that any goal worth achieving will take time. That can be intimidating and even discouraging. Simply setting a goal or committing to a challenge makes you vulnerable because you're admitting you want something enough to risk failure. For many, this combination of vulnerability and discouragement can be so overwhelming that it paralyzes them in fear—leaving them unable to act.

Shortcuts become increasingly attractive in a world that places so many demands on our time and attention. Despite the temptation, they will never provide the same level of fulfillment because the journey is more important than the destination. Life hacks may get you to the endpoint, but they deprive you of all the lessons and experiences. The journey toward our goals is an opportunity to learn, grow, and establish positive habits.

Positive habits are the building blocks of progress. Without them, our aspirations and dreams slowly fade into regret before disappearing altogether. What would happen if you set a goal to lose thirty pounds but refused to change your behavior? That's right, nothing. But, if you choose a more disciplined approach, including regular exercise and eating healthy, in time, those become habits that remain with you for life. Even if I could offer you a pill that guaranteed overnight success, which most people would take, you'd lose those gains as quickly as you got them. You'd continue the same bad habits because there's no substitute for the hard-earned wisdom of experience. The most valuable takeaway from any journey is what you learn along the way.

It's also important to recognize that journeys are rarely linear. It's easy to stay motivated while making clear, steady progress, but things get complicated when you hit peaks, valleys, and the occasional U-turn. You may move forward five feet, back two, then forward one. Despite the setbacks you experience, the most important thing you can do is stay committed and focused.

Consider Alcoholics Anonymous. To the casual observer, AA's 12-step program appears linear, but speak to those with first-hand knowledge, and you'll quickly learn it's circular. Most people who struggle with addiction do not succeed during their first attempt at recovery, so the program uses incremental steps in concert with a cyclical approach. Like sobriety, success is a never-ending process built on daily choices.

An Everyday Warrior recognizes that the long, winding path is part of the process, and the only way forward is to take one step ATTA time.

THE ATTA WAY: PROGRESS OVER PERFECTION

The foundation of the ATTA Way is the idea that success happens one step ATTA time—a concept that centers on five fundamental principles:

1. **Prioritize endurance:** Life isn't an Olympic sport, a professional football game, or a championship

boxing match where victory requires peak performance. Constantly striving for *peak* performance
will only end one way—with you burnt out. Instead,
focus on sustaining *optimal* performance for as
long as possible. When I say optimal performance,
I mean optimal for you, which changes throughout life based on age, fitness level, and knowledge.
Goals take time to achieve, and while it may seem
illogical, focusing on endurance instead of speed
will get you there faster and provide a solid foundation to build upon.

2. **Earn it:** There are no hacks, and looking for a
shortcut will only derail you. When you deviate
from the ATTA Way, you're more likely to waste
time and sacrifice efficiency, effectiveness, and
progress. Even if the journey takes longer than
expected or is more complicated than you expected,
trust yourself and the process. You can't buy
success—you have to earn it.

3. **Focus:** The most challenging part isn't taking the
individual steps. It's the discipline and accountability required to consistently follow through.
Maintaining focus can be difficult because of the
competing demands in our lives. The expectation is
that we multitask to stay on top, but even computers
stop for a nanosecond in between tasks. Taking one
step ATTA time makes us consciously focus on what

truly matters. While distractions are inevitable, your ability to overcome them depends on your resilience, tenacity, and focus.

1. **Expect challenges:** I guarantee you'll experience roadblocks and challenges throughout your journey. That's a part of life. It's understandable to feel overwhelmed, but you must not let those feelings overshadow your approach. Expect to get knocked down, but be ready to bounce back up. Navigating adversity requires breaking things down into smaller pieces and prioritizing them by order of urgency. Take problems one ATTA time, and, before you know it, you'll wonder why you ever felt overwhelmed. We can handle anything life throws at us if we do it the ATTA Way.

2. **Have a warrior mindset:** Warriors recognize that the power of positivity and having belief in ourselves is what gives us the strength to overcome challenges. We know success takes time and humility is essential. We can create something incredible when we recognize our limitations, take small steps, and embrace pragmatism. Being realistic about our abilities is the only way to keep moving and avoid burnout.

In my eyes, the ATTA Way is the most realistic approach available. Whether you're building a business or climbing Mount

Everest, the only way to get where you're going is by taking one step ATTA time.

BREAKING FREE FROM INSTANT GRATIFICATION

A giant obstacle blocking us from fully embracing the effectiveness of the ATTA Way is our desire for instant gratification. The modern world has conditioned us with on-demand entertainment, same-day delivery, and credit cards that allow us to buy what we can't afford. Each time we scroll, eat, play, or shop, we receive a single dose of happiness. These activities cause our brains to release dopamine, the chemical responsible for experiencing joy and pleasure. Social media, entertainment, and shopping platforms invest a lot in the scientific research behind fostering this "need it now" mentality, because our need for instant gratification turns into profits for them. The result is many of us are now addicted to instant gratification.

The "need it now" compulsion can be difficult to break. But, working hard to free yourself is worth it because delaying gratification sustains us in far more significant ways. Giving in to the siren song of instant gratification is easy, but it always comes at a cost. Like a credit card, you get what you want now and pay for it later, with interest. Getting what we want feels great at first, but then the bills pile up, stress increases, and our relationships suffer. Delaying gratification means paying a smaller cost up front in exchange for reaping the long-term rewards.

In the late 1960s, Stanford professor Walter Mischel started a series of groundbreaking psychological studies called the Marshmallow Experiment, the results of which were published in the article "Cognitive and Attentional Mechanisms in Delay of Gratification" in the *Journal of Personality and Social Psychology*. Professor Mischel and his team tested the willpower of hundreds of children between the ages of four and five. The experiment would begin with a researcher bringing a child into a private room, asking them to sit at a table, and placing a marshmallow in front of them. The researcher would then tell the young subject that he'd be right back and ask them not to eat the marshmallow. The researcher would promise the child a second marshmallow if they listened and didn't eat it. Once the researcher stepped out, the child had two options: eat the delicious treat immediately or wait and get two later. While they tried, most children broke down and ate the marshmallow.

Researchers followed the children for more than forty years; what they found made the Marshmallow Experiment famous. The subjects who delayed gratification long enough to earn a second marshmallow scored higher on their SATs, experienced less obesity, and were at a decreased risk of developing substance abuse issues compared to those who opted for instant gratification.

Before you get worried about your little one, we're not saying a four-year-old who fails to pass up a treat is doomed for failure.

However, learning how to resist the trap of instant gratification can improve your chances for overall success and happiness.

Fortunately, there are steps you can take to break free from the instant gratification trap and embrace the ATTA Way:

- **Train:** Strengthen your ability to delay gratification through training. Just as we train our muscles at the gym, you can train your mind to resist daily temptation. Start with something easy to resist. Maybe you suddenly want a new pair of running shoes you see online, and they're only one click away. Make a conscious effort to wait five minutes and tell yourself that you'll buy the shoes when you have the extra money. Soon the urge will subside, and—boom—gratification delayed! The more you do it, the easier it'll become, and the longer you'll be able to delay gratification. Resist the urge one temptation ATTA time!

- **Practice gratitude:** When you appreciate what you have, the urge to acquire more diminishes. Taking stock of your current life strengthens your ability to delay gratification long enough to reach your long-term goals. Wanting a new car is not the problem (we all want new things), but if your long-term goal is buying a house, then spending thousands on a down payment for a car will delay that long-term goal. Achieve great things one moment of gratitude ATTA time!

- **Use reverse planning:** Reverse planning is a project management technique used in business and the military. It's developing a plan by starting with your end goal and working your way backward. This method will help you plan a path to your goal while also identifying critical milestones. Achieving each of these will keep you motivated and add to your momentum. Delayed gratification is far easier when you have a clear path to your goal. Make that plan one milestone ATTA time!

- **Chunk it up:** Chunking is the practice of taking a considerable challenge (or goal) and dividing it into monthly, weekly, and daily steps. An ambitious goal can feel impossible, especially when success is in the distant future. But, setting out to achieve a series of incremental goals keeps you focused by giving you many small victories to celebrate. You can't delay gratification forever, so celebrate one small victory ATTA time!

- **Apply the five-minute rule:** When you're overwhelmed or tempted by instant gratification, stop what you're doing and spend five minutes working toward your goal. Do you want to scroll social media? Read for five minutes. Are you overwhelmed by your messy house? Clean a specific area for five minutes.

Five minutes is such a short amount of time that there's no excuse not to do it. This accomplishment will help you recognize that you're making progress, even if it's five minutes ATTA time!

- **Cultivate habits and build discipline:** Shifting from the toxic cycle of instant gratification to the freedom of the ATTA Way means making your desired behaviors automatic. Accomplishing this requires positive habits and discipline, which we'll discuss in Chapter 9, "The Warrior Way." We all have the ability to develop discipline, and we do it one positive habit ATTA time!

If success were easy, everyone would have it. Whether it's a baseball card or success, value comes from supply and demand. Scarcity is why a Honus Wagner baseball card sold for $6.6 million in 2021, and it's also why achieving success is priceless. If either of these were commonplace, they'd be worthless. But that's the point. When you accept that a goal is worth achieving, you know it won't be easy or happen overnight. That scarcity and difficulty make it far more likely that you'll work hard and recognize the value of each step.

After Action Review

In Chapter 6, "Doing > Talking," you created a SMART goal. Now use chunking to break that goal down into actionable steps, and utilize reverse planning to create a realistic timeline with appropriate milestones along the way to measure your progress toward achieving your goal.

SMART goal:

Timeline of actionable steps and milestones:

Other questions to consider:

- What is the one thing you can do today to get started toward your goal? Not tomorrow, TODAY!

- List areas where you struggle with instant gratification. What are the root causes? How does giving into it make you feel?

- Create an affirmation that you can repeat when you feel the urge to engage in instant gratification.

Key Takeaways

- Changing your life and achieving your goals isn't easy, and it won't happen overnight. But you wouldn't want it to, because then you'd miss out on the experiences and growth along the way.

- Train yourself to avoid instant gratification and realize how much more fulfilling it is to earn something through hard work and dedication.

- No matter where you're going or how long the journey, there's no better approach than taking it one step ATTA time.

8

GET COMFORTABLE WITH BEING UNCOMFORTABLE

The truth is that our finest moments are most likely to occur when we are feeling deeply uncomfortable, unhappy, or unfulfilled. For it is only in such moments, propelled by our discomfort, that we are likely to step out of our ruts and start searching for different ways or truer answers.

—M. SCOTT PECK, psychiatrist and author of The Road Less Traveled

ON JANUARY 24, 2013, THE U.S. MILITARY ANNOUNCED an end to their Combat Exclusion Policy, which prohibited women from serving on the front lines of combat. While this decision was an optical victory, those in the military knew female soldiers had long served in this capacity. Although women could now "officially" serve, they were still excluded from attending the military's top training programs, including Army Ranger School. Considered one of the world's most difficult specialized combat training courses, more than 60% of those who start the grueling 61+ day program fail within the first four days.

When the Army lifted the ban, Lieutenant Colonel Lisa Jaster, then a major, lived in Houston, Texas, with her husband and two small children. The Army Reservist met the criteria for Ranger School but was unsure if she should apply. Even with encouragement from her husband, Marine Colonel Allan Jaster, and senior noncommissioned, Sergeant Major Robby Payne, Lisa was still torn. While the people she respected most told her to go for it, others told her not to.

That all changed when a female friend on Facebook commented, "If you're not there for the little things when your kids are small, they won't come to you with the big things when they grow up." As soon as Lisa read that, she knew what to do. For her, it was about teaching her children that you don't pass up an opportunity simply because it'll be difficult and uncomfortable. Despite their young age, Lisa's children proudly encouraged their mom to go for it.

In 2015, Lisa left her family and career to take her shot at history. The average age of those in Ranger School is twenty-three years old; Lisa began training at thirty-seven. Despite the rigorous twenty-hour days, strict diet, and brutal elements, she refused to quit. After six months, Lisa became the first female Reservist, and one of the first three women in history, to graduate from Ranger School. Lisa is the epitome of what it means to "get comfortable with being uncomfortable." Her story continues inspiring young women for many reasons, including her incredible resolve, discipline, and bravery. Lieutenant Colonel Jaster continues to serve today and recently completed a tour as a battalion commander.

THE VALUE OF DISCOMFORT

A beautiful life is one in which we never stop learning. Does that mean learning is taking comfort in knowledge? No, it's about choosing continuous growth by intentionally placing yourself in situations outside your comfort zone because avoiding discomfort stunts growth and makes room for complacency.

Stress has historically been misunderstood and viewed in a negative light. While experiencing too much stress can harm our mental and physical well-being, some stress is a necessary part of life. Our society, however, encourages working to eliminate all stress at all costs. But having no stress can be just as harmful as having too much. Stress propels growth, which makes it vital that we redefine it and how we manage it.

Stress is just as necessary to build muscle as rest. Our physical, mental, and spiritual health requires stress to grow, followed by short rest and recovery periods. Of course, resting too long invites atrophy, and our physical, mental, and spiritual gains suffer.

Serving in Special Operations taught me that growth and learning occur when you push yourself beyond your limits. The space outside your comfort zone is also where you develop a warrior mindset. When people reach their mental and physical limits, hard skills degrade. For example, if a welder has to work in subzero conditions, they will become mentally and physically stressed. Their hard skills—the abilities they rely on to do their job—will degrade. To complete the work, they'll have to rely on soft skills, such as resilience, drive, and positivity. When you have no choice, you upgrade your soft skills.

"Get comfortable with being uncomfortable" is thus a phrase that was repeated throughout my military training. Some instructors even laughed when they said it, like an inside joke that we hadn't yet earned the right to get. Eventually, I realized they knew something I didn't. They laughed because getting comfortable with being uncomfortable was about more than training.

When you complete the grueling one-year process of becoming a Navy SEAL, you'd think the discomfort would lessen, but it does not. After training, you're continually exposed to stressful, volatile environments designed to push you past your limits. When instructors induce discomfort, it's not a form of hazing; it's a requirement. Getting comfortable with being uncomfortable is a necessity for SEALs and for warriors regardless of their profession.

We all tend to become a little too comfortable in our environment. Even if it's natural, failing to introduce new stimuli (risk, adventure, the unfamiliar) will stunt your growth and make you lose a sense of your capabilities. Worse, comfort can numb your senses. In *The Comfort Crisis*, Michael Easter discusses our evolutionary need for challenges and how discomfort helps us regain perspective and focus. Whether big or small, calculated risks help you find greater happiness and success while increasing your ability to handle situations perceived to be outside of your limits. Studies have shown that leaving our comfort zone increases brain activity, supports learning, and allows us to retain positive emotions and deflect negativity.

As an Everyday Warrior, it's unlikely that you'll find yourself on a literal battlefield, but you are on the front lines of life. Achieving your goals will require some discomfort.

EMBRACING RISK AND VULNERABILITY

For most of us, leaving our comfort zone is problematic due to the risk involved. Humans are naturally risk averse, and we value security, comfort, and peace. As author Aubrey Marcus wrote in *Own the Day, Own Your Life*, "Our...culture is built on the elimination of the difficult and the pursuit of the comfortable." Just because we're inclined to seek comfort doesn't mean we should—after all, growth requires risk.

Special Operators learn to embrace risk because no risk means no reward. Risk is inherent in everything we do, but warriors understand how to mitigate risk, dare greatly, and achieve extraordinary feats.

Challenging ourselves and embracing risk is easier for some than it is for others. If you struggle with this, recognize that pushing ourselves outside of our comfort zone is an acquired skill. Somebody who can enter an uncomfortable situation with humble confidence was most likely not born with that ability but developed it. You can also get comfortable with being uncomfortable by exposing yourself to increasing levels of risk.

You may feel overwhelmed by the very idea of being uncomfortable and seeking risks. Don't be too hard on yourself; we were raised in a comfort-loving society. But, it's time to take ownership. Those feelings will never leave if you don't force them out. Resistance to discomfort often originates in fear. So rather than beating yourself up, figure out why you're afraid. Is it the fear of failing? Of letting someone down? Of facing judgment? Confronting our fears begins with identifying them.

Inviting discomfort requires vulnerability, and much like our response to risk, we instinctively avoid vulnerability. One way we do this is denying that our imperfections exist—even to ourselves. A facade of perfection might keep you comfortable, but the foundation of that facade is not steeped in reality. Anything built on a weak foundation will inevitably crumble. Despite your reasons for resisting, you must find a way to push past your fears to grow and achieve your goals.

PUSH THROUGH THE BOUNDARIES OF FEAR

Think of being comfortable with the uncomfortable as it pertains to parenthood. As parents, our job is to raise children to be strong, independent, and capable adults. Raising them is a delicate balance between not holding on too tight and not letting loose too soon. We want to protect our children from discomfort while not stunting their growth and preventing them from developing independence.

As difficult as it is, we must let our kids make their own mistakes. Despite our worries, making mistakes is the only way for them to learn some of life's most valuable lessons. Likewise, you must seek discomfort, not in spite of but *because of* the risks. Just as you would guide your child and help them avoid needlessly dangerous situations, you can take steps to protect yourself that won't negatively impact your growth.

- **Seek discomfort intentionally:** Fear is the biggest roadblock stopping you from leaving your comfort zone. Author and retired Navy SEAL commander Rich

Diviney explains that fear is a by-product of anxiety and uncertainty. One of the simplest ways to reduce these negative feelings—thus neutralizing fear—is to put yourself in challenging situations intentionally. By building your tolerance to discomfort, you can reduce uncertainty and anxiety and create a greater sense of control. The more you do this, the greater the likelihood of success in volatile, uncertain, and chaotic situations. Fortune favors the prepared. Being prepared doesn't guarantee success, but it puts you in the right mindset for it to happen. So choose discomfort and take steps to increase your tolerance for anxiety and uncertainty—the world is full of it.

- **Challenge your limits:** Like your definition of success, your limits are your own. What's uncomfortable for another person might be perfectly pleasant for you. The point of intentional discomfort is growth, so choose challenges that you know will push you past your limits. Use the weaknesses you identified in Chapter 4, "It Begins and Ends with You," as a starting point; stretch yourself until those liabilities become assets. Also, consider the environments that'll force you to confront and work through those fears.

- **Scale your approach:** There's an old saying, "Every master was once a novice." When exposing yourself to uncomfortable situations, don't start by doing a cannonball dive into the deep end. Instead, dip your toe in the water; knowing the temperature will put you in a better position to scale your exposure. If you're beginning a fitness goal, do not commit yourself to spending three hours in the gym seven days a week. Instead, commit to something more attainable, like one hour in the gym three days a week. Give yourself the time to build a solid foundation. Starting small prevents you from being overwhelmed by the commitment while helping you grow confidence and momentum. Recently, to get myself out of a rut, I decided to go skydiving in the Mount Everest region, which includes some of the highest drop zones in the world. Normal skydives are around twelve thousand feet; these jumps were as high as twenty-three thousand feet and required oxygen. While that certainly pulled me out of my comfort zone, pushing your limits doesn't have to be that drastic; it can be finding little ways to embrace discomfort each day. If you hate public speaking, consider standing up at a work meeting to speak about an issue that matters to you. Or take a more literal approach to discomfort and try sitting in an ice bath for one to two minutes a day and build from there—that's guaranteed to make anyone uncomfortable.

- **Recognize little successes:** Whether you realize it or not, you've taken risks in your life. Take time to recognize your efforts, even the small ones. Perhaps you met someone who shares all your interests after you forced yourself to attend a social event you were dreading. Even when the outcome of a risk doesn't turn out favorable, you usually still gain valuable lessons. Maybe you took a chance at work by volunteering for a new project that you didn't end up enjoying. At least you learned what kind of work is most fulfilling—a lesson you otherwise wouldn't have had if you remained wrapped in your comfort zone. Reflecting on what you gained during past moments of discomfort will help you build the confidence to take future risks.

- **Remember, you're not alone:** Discomfort and risk are not necessarily solo ventures, and those around you can help with your journey. Often, the fear of vulnerability stops us from reaching out. We may not want to admit we're uncomfortable, but we need to realize that everyone experiences these feelings. Opening up and asking for help can calm the fear of risk.

- **Track your growth:** While pushing yourself outside your comfort zone is never easy, it helps to see your progress. We tend to finish things, forget about them, and move on. Because of this, we never fully realize the improvement we've made. Journaling is an excellent tool for tracking growth. In addition to keeping you focused and goal-oriented, you'll have a written record of how far you've come and a way to recalibrate your strengths and weaknesses as they change.

- **Practice and then practice more:** Getting comfortable with being uncomfortable is an acquired skill that becomes easier with practice. For example, public speaking used to make me slightly uncomfortable. That's a lie—it actually terrified me! It was so bad that even addressing my SEAL Team filled me with fear. But I realized that if I wanted to convey my points and impact lives, I had to get over my discomfort and sharpen my skills. While it was a rocky journey, I now regularly speak in front of audiences as large as twenty-five thousand people. The more uncomfortable the environments you place yourself in, the calmer you become. Even if the fear and anxiety never entirely subside, you know you're in control of them, not the other way around.

Even with these strategies in your arsenal, going outside of your comfort zone will still be uncomfortable—that's the point. Deliberately exposing yourself to discomfort builds your endurance and resilience. In the military, we train by repeatedly running through the same movements until we can do them blindfolded—then we keep doing it. This is because we fight how we train. When the time comes to do it for real, we need the muscle memory built during training to kick in. By practicing deliberate discomfort, when life throws you face-first into moments of unplanned discomfort (which it will), you'll be ready, in control, and you'll fight how you trained.

There are two options when it comes to taking risks: avoidance and discovery. Avoid trying things and you'll never know yourself the way you want to. After all, it's a big world out there. On the other hand, discovering something that fulfills you and helps you grow will lead to greater happiness. Do you want to live your life running from risks and discomfort or toward your goals and aspirations? Well, guess what: all four of those are in the same direction.

After Action Review

- List areas in your life where you've become too comfortable. What has allowed you to grow this complacent?

- What prevents you from taking risks and being vulnerable?

- Is the fear of failure holding you back? What do you fear most about failure? What's your plan for overcoming failure?

- What is a small step you can take each day to increase your risk tolerance?

Key Takeaways

- Comfort may be appealing in the moment, but in the long term it's stymieing growth and encouraging atrophy. We need to experience discomfort to reach our potential.

- Embrace risk and vulnerability because these are essential for achieving any goal. Experiencing intentional discomfort today will help you navigate away from unexpected discomfort tomorrow.

- Comfort zones are bound by fear, but when we begin to identify and address those fears, we expand our comfort zones and build our tolerance for discomfort.

9

THE WARRIOR WAY: GET SHIT DONE. MAKE SHIT HAPPEN. DO IT ALL AGAIN TOMORROW.

Discipline is choosing between what you want now and what you want most.

—ABRAHAM LINCOLN

WHEN JULIANE GALLINA WAS SEVEN YEARS OLD, HER FATHER, a former Manhattan assistant district attorney, was murdered in what newspapers called a "mob-style attack." Although she didn't know it, this horrific tragedy would shape her life, mold her character, and factor into her decision to live a life of honor and integrity. The loss of her father weighed heavy on young Juliane. Thankfully her mother, a public school librarian in the South Bronx, and siblings provided one another with emotional support. While they had each other to lean on, money was tight and would remain so for much of her young life.

At fourteen years old, Juliane was doing so well in school that a guidance counselor told her she could be anything she wanted. It was at that moment she decided to be an astronaut. After learning that naval aviation was her best path to success, Juliane shifted her focus to developing leadership skills in preparation for the military.

Four years later, those in her class were busy applying to their first-, second-, and third-choice colleges, but Juliane only applied to one: the U.S. Naval Academy in Annapolis, Maryland. With women only making up 10% of each incoming class, everyone accepted that the odds were stacked against her—everyone but Juliane. Having spent her entire high school career putting in the work and holding herself accountable, she was confident that her preparation would equate to success. She was right. While she expected to get in, she was unprepared for what happened next. Instead of congratulating her and offering their support, the faculty at her high school pushed back against her plans. This included a history teacher who told her she wasn't suited for the military and tried talking her into attending a liberal arts school instead.

Juliane knew they were wrong and set out to prove it. Three years later, she did just that when she became the first female brigade commander in the U.S. Naval Academy's 161-year history. While it's an incredible honor, this student-leadership position is also an immense responsibility. Along with the regular stress of the role, being the first woman to serve as brigade commander meant Juliane had to shoulder the unique challenge of dealing with those skeptical of her ability to execute the required duties. But the forty-three hundred midshipmen under her charge, the Naval Academy leadership, and the world quickly learned what Juliane had always known: she was more than ready.

Then, Juliane received a devastating blow in her senior year when she failed to meet the Navy's pilot height requirement by 1.1 inches. The dream she'd chased for eight years was suddenly over, and she was at a crossroads. She could become filled with resentment and spite, or she could get back up, reflect, and move forward. There was but one choice for Juliane, a woman who'd built her life around honor and integrity. Move forward and graduate. Due to her academic performance and leadership credentials, the Navy sent her to graduate school to earn her master's degree in space systems operations and national reconnaissance. While there, she decided to expand her studies and earned a second master's in electrical engineering.

She went on to have an incredible career. Then after twenty-two years of service, Lieutenant Commander Gallina retired from the Navy. Her retirement closed an important chapter of her life, but it was far from the end of her story. From there, she served ten years with the National Reconnaissance Office—first as a senior systems engineer and then as the deputy program director—before working as a high-level IBM executive for nine years. After her decade-long detour in the private sector, Juliane's love for public service brought her to the Central Intelligence Agency (CIA), where she held the title of chief information officer for three years. She continues a proud tradition of service as the CIA's associate deputy director for digital innovation.

Losing a parent the way Juliane did is something no child should have to endure. While we may not have much control over what life throws at us, one thing we can control is our response. Juliane turned the worst possible situation into the impetus of an extraordinary career of service and leadership. When she wiped her tears away following the loss of her father, seven-year-old Juliane Gallina was preparing to make history—she just didn't know it yet.

THE WARRIOR CODE

Whether we realize it or not, we all live by a code. It may be a structured set of moral guidelines dictating how we live, as is the case with organized religion, or an adopted motto that provides us direction and clarity, such as *carpe diem*. Even those who believe they don't follow a code, in fact do. Maybe they abide by their family's customs or follow the laws of their community—these are also codes. Codes are important to the collective because, without them, society breaks down. They're also crucial for individuals because they create a sense of belonging, help us maintain our principles, and are powerful tools for achieving success.

As Everyday Warriors, we live by a code that's simple to understand, easy to implement, yet challenging to master. It's one that Juliane Gallina, and warriors like her, have instinctively followed without even realizing it. While they may not have been able to put it into words, they certainly felt it—because it's a code that embodies the very willpower, determination, and grit that define the warrior spirit:

The Warrior Way: Get Shit Done. Make Shit Happen. Do It All Again Tomorrow.

Each part is built upon a different warrior principle:

1. **Get Shit Done:** We must develop the discipline and accountability to do what it takes to accomplish our goals, even when we don't feel like it. This takes time, dedication, and the commitment to recover from slipups when they happen.

2. **Make Shit Happen:** We must be ready to seize opportunities without being told—this requires a bias for action. It also means avoiding excuses; if we want something bad enough, we make shit happen.

3. **Do It All Again Tomorrow:** When it comes to achieving success, there's nothing more powerful than building positive habits. Developing these healthy behaviors is the key to the Warrior Way.

GET SHIT DONE

Discipline isn't something you either have or don't. By definition, it's training people to follow the rules or adhere to a code using corrective action. Thus, discipline isn't something you're born with; it's something you develop one step ATTA time.

In the simplest terms, you develop discipline through commitment. Each day, you make the hard choices that get you closer to your goals. Whether working out, avoiding junk food, or practicing a new skill, you build discipline by remaining accountable until those choices become a habit. Of course, that's easier said than done.

Here are five tips for getting shit done:

- **Make a plan:** Most of us are stretched thin between work, family, and life. If you have a lot on your plate, it's easy to make excuses. So, you can't expect to become disciplined without planning. Start by identifying your priorities. Pick one or two areas where you want to be more disciplined, then decide what you will do and when. Set aside five minutes each morning to prepare for a disciplined day and five minutes each evening to journal about what you've learned on your journey to becoming a better warrior.

- **Remember the big picture:** The biggest reason people fail to reach their goals is that they forget. As an Everyday Warrior, vow to never forget the big picture or why you started the journey. Splurging on an unnecessary purchase might not seem like a big deal, but it is. Reminding yourself that you're saving for your kid's college fund, a down payment on a house, a big vacation, a new car, or whatever it is you want will make you think twice about swiping that credit card. Keep a list of your goals somewhere you'll see them. Reminders on your phone's home screen or refrigerator will help keep you grounded and focused.

- **Measure your discipline:** In *Measure What Matters*, John Doerr explains that what we measure is what we get done. Just like you measure your progress toward your goals, you want to measure your discipline. Consider using a tracking system like a habit-tracking app, or design your own using a journal or a spreadsheet. Maybe you only complete your desired activity 25% of the time during your first month but 33% during the second. That's growth! The more aware you are of what you want

149

to do—and what you are doing—the more likely it is that you will keep going.

- **Make discipline your identity:** Who we think we are has a massive impact on our behavior. You are not who you *say* you are—you are what you *do*. It takes discipline to say *no* to unhealthy habits and engage in positive ones. Think of yourself as a disciplined person, and you'll subconsciously move in that direction. Start by making discipline a part of your identity. Adopt this internal monologue as your mantra: "I'm an Everyday Warrior who makes the tough choices and takes the hard steps needed to succeed."

- **Reward yourself:** Discipline is hard work, so give yourself breaks. Even fitness experts incorporate a cheat day into their schedule to eat their favorite guilty pleasure foods. If you make your discipline journey all or nothing, you'll be miserable and likely end up with nothing. You're more likely to succeed if you build in breaks and celebrate milestones. Remember, the goal is sustained optimal performance—not perfection.

There are no shortcuts because discipline is not a destination; it's a way of life that ebbs and flows as circumstances change and as you grow. That's okay because the goal is continual improvement, and that's precisely what you'll achieve.

DISCIPLINE TRAINING WHEELS

I've served with incredible individuals who take self-discipline to another level—but they didn't start out that way. I certainly didn't. Before becoming a Marine, I led an undisciplined life, barely graduated from high school, dropped out of college, and was kicked out of ROTC. It's an understatement to say that I lacked the positive habits necessary for success. But the military changed me; the three months I spent in boot camp reengineered my mindset and outlook on life. I learned to lead a disciplined life from one of the world's most effective, efficient, and disciplined organizations—the United States Marine Corps.

For example, drill instructors required us to make our beds to an exacting standard each morning. A neatly made bed, complete with hospital corners, was far from the point. It's about discipline and holding ourselves to a higher standard, engaging in routine behaviors, and creating neural pathways in our brains. Admiral McRaven, Navy SEAL and former Commander of the U.S. Special Operations Command, famously called it the "first victory of the day." He said that no matter how good or bad his day was, returning to a neatly made bed each night reminded him that he started his day with a victory. It allowed him to fall asleep with a sense of accomplishment, regardless of how his day had been.

There are two lessons here. First, although self-discipline is the goal, starting with discipline from an external source can help you internalize crucial habits. You should not rely on others to maintain your discipline long-term, but you can use them as metaphorical training wheels while getting your balance. While I no longer need Marine Corps drill instructors watching my every move, they certainly played a significant role in helping me internalize discipline. Second, no rule says discipline must start with some massive undertaking, like waking up before sunrise. Another way to use training wheels is by focusing on small actions, like making your bed each morning. Sometimes, that's all it takes for your discipline to grow. Before you know it, you're flying down a hill before you even realize that your training wheels are gone.

WHAT TO DO WHEN YOUR DISCIPLINE SLIPS

The question isn't whether your discipline will slip, because nobody can maintain perfect discipline, but what you'll do when it does. To help prevent slips, I take regular discipline breaks in business, fitness, diet, and every other part of my life. That helps, but guess what: *I still slip up occasionally.*

We are each responsible for maintaining our own discipline, which means there's nobody to blame when we fall short. We must take a hard look at ourselves and admit when we mess up—and let me reiterate, we all mess up! That part is inevitable, but recognizing it and holding ourselves accountable is where growth happens.

Here's a six-step recovery process for when your discipline slips:

1. **Recognize that you slipped and why:** You know when your discipline slips—if you don't, you're lying to yourself. One of my weaknesses is Crumbl Cookies, a national bakery that delivers freshly baked cookies to your doorstep. As I scarf down three thousand calories of cookie goodness at 9 p.m., I'm not thinking, "Man, I'm killing it with my diet." I know I've messed up. When this happens to you, try to figure out why you slipped. Maybe you were stressed at work, or perhaps your routine changed and disrupted your habits. The better you recognize your triggers, the faster you'll be at identifying and preventing future slipups.

2. **Don't look at it as a zero-sum game:** Developing discipline is a process. Don't treat a slipup as a total loss. The failure doesn't happen when you're eating the cookie. It happens a moment later when you say, "Well, I've already failed...might as well keep going," and then devour fifteen more. Recognize a lapse of discipline for what it is: a single slipup, not a complete failure.

3. **Hold yourself accountable:** Accountability is not about punishing yourself. The most challenging parts of life are inevitable, so we must be practical and recognize we can't give 100% all the time. Simultaneously, we must also acknowledge that we can make progress. In 2006, grenade shrapnel tore thirty holes in my legs. I'm here today because Master-at-Arms Second Class Michael A. Monsoor (SEAL) jumped on the grenade, saving my life and the lives of two other SEALs. In 2008, he was posthumously awarded the Medal of Honor for his selfless actions on that late September day. I was physically fit when I was wounded, but after months of painful rehab and eating a steady diet of Chinese food, McDonald's, and Jack Daniels, I went from a solid 185 pounds to a soft 215. Holding myself accountable meant recognizing that I could have controlled my diet even if I couldn't control my injury. Hold yourself accountable by paying attention to how you feel after falling short. Then, the next time you're struggling, remind yourself how bad it feels to slip.

4. **Adjust (if necessary):** Sometimes we overestimate our capabilities and take on too much. If you set an outrageous goal, you're setting yourself up for failure. Scale back if necessary. Pragmatic goal setting is a skill that comes with experience, as does understanding your strengths and limitations.

5. **Get back on track, quickly:** Discipline is about resiliency. You will get knocked off track; what matters is that you quickly get back up. Whether you're off for a day, month, or year, it's never too late. Don't waste another day! After my injury in 2006, I started working on becoming disciplined again. It took a solid two years, but eventually, I was in the best shape of my life. The hardest part of self-discipline is starting over again when you fail. Plan now so you're ready to get back on track when it happens.

6. **Limit future slips:** Once you know your triggers, you can work to prevent future slips. I recently had a hip replacement. Before the surgery, I made a plan to help avoid another lapse in discipline. I knew I'd be spending a lot of time on the couch recovering, so I focused on the one thing I could control: my diet. I still gained some weight, but thanks to the careful attention I paid to what I was eating, the gain was minimal compared to 2006. As a result, getting back into shape was much easier and faster.

Slipups are unavoidable. Life will throw you curveballs, your priorities will shift, and you will fall out of habits. Don't bother trying to control things you can't. Instead, focus on what you can, like being more disciplined moving forward. If you miss the gym for a week, don't let it turn into a month. If you lose touch with a good friend for a year, don't let it turn into two. Hold yourself accountable and get shit done.

MAKE SHIT HAPPEN

As a child, Juliane could have reacted to the tragedy by giving up—the way many people three times her age do when faced with far less. But that's not what she did as a young girl, a teen, or an adult. No matter what others said, she followed her own path.

We all know that making excuses seems far easier than putting in the work. Too many fall into this trap; they blame their lack of achievement on circumstances beyond their control. They make excuses instead of making shit happen. They're either too young or too old, too broke or too late. If they had a bias for action, like Juliane, they'd plan, prepare, and execute...no matter what. The idea of making shit happen is all about not having what you need to do something but figuring it out and getting it done anyway. Juliane could have sat back and made excuses on why she couldn't achieve her dreams.

In fact, let's come up with some she could have used.

- My mom needs me at home.

- I'm too sad about my dad to even try.

- Life's not fair.

- I probably won't get into the Naval Academy because I'm a woman.

156

- My high school teacher said I shouldn't do it.

- I want to hang out with my friends instead of studying.

- I made it all this way, but I'm not tall enough.

I could keep going, but you get the idea. No matter what life threw at Juliane, she dealt with it like a true warrior. Regardless of how valid they may sound and who accepts them, they are still not reasons—they're excuses. It's time to take action and *make shit happen!*

DO IT ALL AGAIN TOMORROW

Warriors don't just get shit done and make shit happen. They do it repeatedly, again and again and again. Life doesn't stop, and they don't either. This is the real key to discipline: you can't just do the right thing today; you have to do it again tomorrow. Your biggest ally here is positive habits.

Habits are recurring patterns of behavior formed through repetition that allow us to perform regular tasks with little effort or conscious thought. You may not realize it, but you rely on habits all day long; this includes the time you wake up each morning, how you put your socks on, and even the route you drive to work. Our brains cannot think about every action we perform, so things we do repeatedly go on autopilot. While they appear to be set in stone, they're not. The truth is you have the power to improve your life by changing what you do. The more positive behaviors that become habits, the easier maintaining discipline is.

Building healthy habits is a process we can break into simple steps. *Atomic Habits* author James Clear explains that habits are feedback loops with four parts: cue, craving, response, and reward. Feedback loops can be negative or positive. Here's an example of each:

Negative feedback loop:

1. **Cue:** Your alarm goes off in the morning.

2. **Craving:** You've slept eight hours but want more sleep.

3. **Response:** You reach over and hit the snooze button.

4. **Reward:** You get unnecessary sleep and reinforce a harmful habit.

Positive feedback loop:

1. **Cue:** Your alarm goes off ten feet from your bed.

2. **Craving:** You want the energized feeling that comes with exercise.

3. **Response:** You immediately get out of bed and turn the alarm off.

4. **Reward:** You exercise, feel good all day, and reinforce a positive habit.

The habits you develop come down to what you want more, which in this case was a choice between extra sleep or feeling energized. Your response to such a craving is a subconscious manifestation of what you desire and value more.

Creating positive habits that help you achieve your goals is about knowing your mind and working within its limitations. When cultivating a new habit, follow these guidelines:

- **Start small:** Select a habit you'd like to develop, but make sure it's realistic and attainable. Let's say you've never meditated before but want to introduce the practice into your life. Beginning with a half hour each day is overly ambitious and increases the likelihood that you'll quit. Instead, set a smaller goal you can maintain, such as devoting five minutes daily. Choosing a time you can manage builds your confidence and sets you up for success. As you gain experience and a better understanding of your strengths, the size and scope of your new habits will undoubtedly grow and increase in complexity.

- **Use your routine as an anchor:** Investing in
  ourselves is exciting, but sometimes the euphoria
  of self-improvement can cause us to go to extremes.
  This can manifest in many ways, including rearrang-
  ing our entire life until it revolves around the new
  habit. This is disruptive. Habits should not be chosen
  or implemented based on emotion or whim. Instead,
  connect them to your existing routine in a seamless
  way. Maybe it's going for a jog in the morning after
  you wake up, meditating for fifteen minutes before
  lunch, or journaling each night after brushing your
  teeth. Anchoring the new habit to something you
  already do—waking up, eating lunch, brushing your
  teeth—goes back to the cue part of the feedback loop
  and will lead you to success.

- **Make success easier:** Do you remember the Staples
  commercial where someone struggles with a task
  until they press the easy button? There may not be an
  easy button in real life, but this step is close. Making
  it easy on yourself by taking simple steps can make a
  big difference in following through. Want to go to the
  gym in the morning? Lay out your workout clothes
  the night before. Want to take a multivitamin every
  day? Put it next to your toothbrush. Want to invest
  more time in fostering friendships? Schedule a calendar reminder that prompts you to call. The easier you
  make a habit in advance, the greater the likelihood of
  following through when the time comes.

- **Reward yourself:** Rewards are a crucial part of the habit loop. They can release dopamine in our brains and make us want to continue. Sometimes the habit itself is rewarding, like how exercising releases endorphins. If it's not, add a reward afterward, like:

  * Enjoying a cheat meal after five days of strict dieting

  * Sleeping in on Saturday after waking up early all week

  * Going on a vacation after the completion of a long project

  * Taking weekends off from the gym after working out every weekday

- **Repeat, repeat, repeat:** Actions become habits through repetition—and lots of it. When starting a new habit, a good rule of thumb is to commit yourself for thirty days. That's because, in those thirty days, there will be enough repetition to turn that activity into a habit.

Habits are at the core of who you are—whether they're positive or negative is entirely up to you. Introducing a new one is difficult, but soon you'll forget you're even doing it. In fact, it'll become such a normal part of life that missing your morning run or afternoon journal entry will leave you feeling off-balance. It's just as crucial to break free from bad habits that are not helping you better yourself. While humans naturally gravitate toward patterns and routines, focus on being more intentional about creating habits that serve your goals instead of hold you back.

After Action Review

- Do you consider yourself a disciplined or undisciplined person?

- Do you continually fail to achieve personal goals? If so, why do you believe that is?

- When you fail, do you hold yourself accountable?

- How will you hold yourself accountable in the future?

- Is there someone who can help keep you accountable initially?

- What small steps can you take to turn negative habits into positive habits?

- How can you adopt the Warrior Way into your daily life?

- Are you ready to Get Shit Done, Make Shit Happen, and Do It All Again Tomorrow? If so, what will you get done and make happen today? How about tomorrow?

Key Takeaways

- The Warrior Way: Get Shit Done. Make Shit Happen. Do It All Again Tomorrow.

- Discipline is a challenge for everyone, but just because it's hard doesn't mean it's impossible. Each of us has the potential to change the way we think about discipline and accountability.

- It is never the wrong time to start working toward becoming more disciplined. Building positive habits is all about cues, self-awareness, and repetition.

- Missteps are a part of the process, and we can't expect perfection. Continuously striving toward progress is the way to maintain your momentum toward your goals.

10

WE ALL NEED A TRIBE—HOMECOMING AND BELONGING

If you hang around five confident people, you will be the sixth. If you hang around five intelligent people, you will be the sixth. If you hang around five millionaires, you will be the sixth. If you hang around five negative people, you will be the sixth.

—AUTHOR UNKNOWN

A HARVARD BUSINESS SCHOOL PROFESSOR TOLD WILL DEAN, founder of Tough Mudder, that no one would pay money to crawl through mud, traverse insane obstacles, or endure painful ice baths. So, what did he do? He responded like a true entrepreneur by setting out to prove the professor wrong—and he did just that. However, it wasn't the obstacles or ice baths that turned Tough Mudder into a $100-million-a-year business; it was something far more primal. Will tapped into the human desire to belong, share adversity, and create a tribal mentality. Maslow's hierarchy of needs speaks to our desire to be a part of something bigger than ourselves. Will Dean not only knew this, but he was able to capitalize on it. The results speak for themselves. Each year, millions of people from around the world pay to be part of his community and feel a sense of belonging they couldn't otherwise find.

We all long for kinship, affiliation, and belonging. In a world where true connection is becoming increasingly rare, people compensate by turning to social media. We should be reaching out to others instead of searching for comfort by staring into a black glass screen. Facebook's 2.9 billion users are individuals desperately trying to connect and belong.

We can't wait for someone to make things better—it's up to us. Go out of your way to be kind; help that elderly stranger get to his flight on time or hold the door open for the person behind you. You know that people are longing for connection... so connect. In doing so, you will help not just others, but yourself too, because nothing great, including your personal goals, is achieved alone. Everyone needs a tribe.

THE POWER OF TRIBES

Hollywood loves the lone wolf narrative—a single person who somehow manages to win despite the insurmountable odds and overwhelming force levied against them. In reality, both wolves and people travel in packs. You will never find an Army Green Beret, Special Reconnaissance Airman, or Navy SEAL running into battle alone unless something has gone terribly wrong. Why is the foundation of Special Operations built around the team, not the individual? Because the most remarkable successes—whether in the military, sports, business, or life—are achieved through the power of the tribe.

If you're trying to be the smartest person in the room by mentioning dominant individual sport athletes like Michael Phelps, Serena Williams, Usain Bolt, Kelly Slater, or Floyd Mayweather Jr. and how they have achieved success on their own—stop, you are wrong. All those amazing athletes are a product of their tribes—parents, coaches, mentors, peers, and loved ones. And no, I hate to break it to you, but Rambo wasn't real. In reality *Rambo* would have been a very short film, and there wouldn't have been a *Rambo 2* through *Rambo 5*. Even Medal of Honor recipients in the military were enabled by amazing teammates.

The most significant wealth of knowledge on success and inspiration exists within the collective group, which I call a tribe. Why are tribes so powerful? When you surround yourself with people you aspire to be like, you're setting yourself up for success. A tribe looks out for one another's best interests and wants nothing but success, happiness, and prosperity for its members. Success from others (our tribe) leaves breadcrumbs. They show the process and procedure that lead to success. That's the power of a good tribe. In fact, Proverbs 27:17 tells us, "As iron sharpens iron, so one person sharpens another." Your tribe reflects your values and makes you who you are. The qualities of those around you can be contagious. If you surround yourself with confident people, your confidence will increase. If you spend time with successful people, soon enough, you will begin to see success. The opposite effect is also true: If you surround yourself with negative people, you will adopt a negative outlook on life. If you spend your time with underachievers, you will likely fall short of your goals.

The right tribe can be the most effective support mechanism. In the business world, when an organization sets a goal, management creates a plan of action and ensures everyone understands the steps to reach that goal. That same process can work in our personal lives. By sharing your plan for achieving your goals with your tribe, you open yourself up to accountability and support. They can advise you, monitor your progress, and provide the wake-up calls you need to remain accountable.

Tribes are particularly critical for your spiritual fitness. When you learn to identify with the successes and failures of your group, you develop selflessness—one of life's most virtuous attributes. As a tribe member, you recognize that it's not all about you; it's about what's best for the team. A tribe mentality translates into serving others and the community, a vital element in our journey toward spiritual fitness. We can achieve far more together, and a tribe helps us have the most significant impact possible and build a legacy that future generations can learn from.

In Chapter 5, "Fighting the Epidemic of Victimhood," I discussed the importance of taking ownership of your life and fighting your own battles. But it's also crucial to understand that not even the most highly skilled warriors fight alone; they lean on their tribes. Taking ownership also means setting yourself up for success—finding the right tribe does precisely that.

THE DISAPPEARANCE OF TRIBES

The psychological need to belong is encoded deep within our DNA, but tribes seem to be rapidly disappearing. In her article "Finding Your Tribe," Psychologist Lauren Woolley, PhD, explains the genesis of tribes, saying, "We are born wired for connection. When our ancestors roamed the land for food, moving in numbers was vital for survival. Early settlers in the United States also had to rely on each other to survive the harsh weather and living conditions." If tribes were so instrumental to survival, why the decline? Dr. Woolley believes the rise of American prosperity meant that we no longer relied on each other for basic survival. Just as atrophy sets in when muscles are not used, tribes deteriorate for much the same reason. But while tribes may not be necessary for our physical survival, they're more crucial than ever for our well-being and success.

The world we live in makes being part of a tribe more challenging. Environmental factors contribute to this, including over-
scheduling and frequent relocation. Moving from city to city and
job to job can make it difficult to build strong community roots.

Technology has fundamentally changed how we interact with
each other and form relationships. We now have the ability to
stay connected regardless of distance. This makes it easier to
maintain relationships and can even broaden a tribe's impact.
But social media has also reinforced the idea that the quantity
of relationships matters more than the quality; simply look at
the social status given to those who amass millions of followers. While technology can supplement relationships, it's far
from a replacement. Our souls are revitalized by the physical
presence of other people.

Perhaps the most disastrous ramifications of these social platforms are deepening fractures across our society. The republic
is painted in a level of division never before experienced within
our lifetime. Political fervor and religious zeal are nothing
new, but the introduction of wokeism, a radical ideology that
demands subservience in thought, word, and deed, directly
contradicts our nation's founding principles. You'd think the
constant access to news and information would help us relate
to one another and bring us closer together. Instead, people
retreat into self-imposed echo chambers where they only
listen to those who agree with them. This refusal to acknowledge the right of others to hold different views and beliefs
has sown strife, fostered discord, and allowed disharmony to

seep into everyday life. Instead of focusing on how we're 80% alike, people are encouraged to separate based on identity and hyper-focus on the other 20%. Compounding the problem, much of the entertainment, media, and advertising we're exposed to each day (both online and off) has been designed to force us into silos. Because the need to belong is in our DNA, we form unnatural tribes based purely on politics, identity, consumer habits, and even hashtags. However, the tribes that serve an Everyday Warrior are built organically through relationships, mutual values, and respect.

All of these challenges make finding your tribe significantly more important.

GOOD TRIBES VS. BAD TRIBES

While it's true that the likelihood of success diminishes without a tribe, it's also important to remember that not all tribes are created equal. Good tribes support you, help you achieve your goals, and promote a positive mindset. On the opposite end of the spectrum, there are bad tribes; they pull you down, keep you stuck in unhealthy habits, and unite against a person, group, or belief.

Characteristics of a good tribe:

- Overwhelmingly positive

- Full of emotional intimacy and vulnerability

- Supportive and focused on accountability

- Actively pushing you to be your best

- Low drama

Characteristics of a bad tribe:

- Extreme negativity

- Excessive dogma and narrow-mindedness

- Unsupportive of other tribe members' goals

- Focused on the individual rather than the team

- Unified against a person, group, or belief

- High drama and jealousy

In theory, we all want a good tribe, but we have a tendency to seek out relationships by reaching down instead of up. It's easy when you're the smartest, best-looking, or most successful person in the group, and it's scary to find your way into a high-performing group where you're no longer the leader. But you'll only grow by surrounding yourself with people who challenge you, whether it's physically, mentally, or spiritually.

While in the military, I was surrounded by men and women who were faster, stronger, tactically superior, and far better leaders. But, as if through osmosis, I absorbed their discipline, accountability, habits, and lessons, which eventually made me a better person. It can be uncomfortable to face your shortcomings, but this isn't a competition. The only person you're competing against is the person you were yesterday. How do you beat them? You let go of the ego and arrogance, get comfortable being uncomfortable, and surround yourself with other Everyday Warriors who challenge you to grow bigger instead of making you feel small.

WHEN TO SAY GOODBYE
TO YOUR TRIBE

To truly begin anew, we must start fresh. One of the most critical parts of finding a good tribe is saying goodbye to the bad one. While it may be necessary, that doesn't make it any less challenging. We all have friendships that have run their course, but we may not know how to sever those ties—even if it's in our best interest. Saying goodbye to old friends is saying goodbye to comfort and familiarity. It can bring up feelings of guilt, grief, and loss; not unlike breaking up with a romantic partner.

As painful as it is when our tribes no longer serve us, we need to move on, especially when they're actively working against our goals.

After I got out of the military, I went from not having a drink in three years to drinking almost every night. Most of it happened at bars with a specific group. They had a lot going for them—they were fun, intelligent, and great people—but their social lives revolved around the bar. I realized that was not an atmosphere where I could move past my challenges.

Eventually, I separated from them. It wasn't because I no longer liked them as people; it was that the environment they inhabited was not conducive to my goals or my health. I had to remove myself from that situation and leave those relationships behind. I had to say goodbye to my tribe.

FINDING AND GROWING YOUR TRIBE

We all have more than one tribe in our life—each serves a different purpose. In my life, there are three distinctive tribes: my immediate family, the SEAL Teams, and my business associates. Certain tribes fit specific aspects of your life, and that's how it should be. The more connections and relationships you build, the more you grow.

To find your tribe, you must be open to new things, venture outside your comfort zone, and accept risk. We tend to build relationships with similar people, but we all have different circumstances, experiences, and perspectives. Make an effort to meet new people and learn from their experiences. When you're open-minded, you set yourself up for maximum growth. Rather than just choosing people who look, think, and act like you, seek those with a similar ethos and moral compass but who offer a different perspective.

I've chosen to surround myself with high-performing individuals who love to lift up others. Someone's personality and mindset are much more important to me than their profession or background. I seek out people who share the attributes I identify with or want to cultivate, like drive and introspection. I also try to augment my tribes with those who can help me learn and grow. If I want to become a better writer, I'll seek out talented writers; if I struggle in an area, I'll find people to offset that weakness.

Most importantly, those in your tribe need to be people you enjoy and like. If you don't naturally desire to spend time with them, the tribe will never be a source of motivation and support. In my experience, an unseen force often brings the right people into your life at the right time. Like romantic relationships, pay attention to whether there's chemistry; the first time I met my friends and tribe, I knew there was a connection within the first five minutes. It should be that effortless.

Tribes are not static; they'll ebb and flow throughout life as you grow and change. For your tribes to remain effective, work to expand them continuously. There are two ways to do this. First, extend yourself into another tribe—the more connections you build, the more relationships you'll have. Second, invite others into your tribe because many people are looking for a tribe, and keeping yourself open to others is one of the best ways to make an impact.

SERVE THE TRIBE, NOT YOURSELF

Being part of a tribe isn't just about what you get; it's about the value you provide the group. Relationships are two-way streets, and your goal is to be an asset to your tribe. Here are a few key traits to focus on to ensure you're giving more than you're taking:

- **Listen more than you talk:** Paying attention enables you to help the tribe and its members. If you're always talking, it means you're not listening and not bringing value. Your relationships with individual members and your standing within the group will suffer.

- **Provide support:** There is strength in numbers, but only when everyone plays their part. When you recognize where you can help others, don't just say you'll support them—take action. If a member starts a new business, be their first customer and spread the word. Recognize that their success is your success.

- **Embrace honesty:** The truth isn't always comfortable, but we owe it to the members of our tribe. If you see someone making a mistake that you can help them avoid, speak up. If you approach it with compassion, care, and kindness, they will value your help rather than see it as criticism.

- **Focus on empathy:** Embracing the perspective and experiences of others gives you the ability to learn from them. By understanding and learning from others, you grow to better understand yourself. Aligning yourself with the tribe will improve your relationships across the board.

- **Transfer knowledge:** Pass knowledge gained from one arena to the next. I might take something from my work tribe, bring it to my family tribe, and say, "Hey, look what I learned." Someone from that family tribe might then share that with another one of their tribes. Sharing fosters relationships, strengthens bonds, and creates tribes of people ready to spread valuable knowledge.

In 1963, President John F. Kennedy shared the long-standing aphorism, "A rising tide lifts all boats." When it comes to your tribe, be that tide of positivity that lifts your friends and helps them on their journeys. When you focus on the group instead of yourself, you automatically help everyone—including you.

After Action Review

- List the tribes in which you belong (e.g., family, social, work, recreation).

- Identify the role of each tribe and its impact on your life (good and bad).

- Which tribes provide the most long-term value (e.g., learning, growth, emotional support, sense of belonging)?

- Which tribes have a negative impact on you, and how? Can you break free from them?

- Are there areas of your life that can improve should you be surrounded by the right tribe (based on common interests, religion, profession, etc.)?

- If so, where can you find this tribe, and what steps will you take to join the group?

Key Takeaways

- None of us are meant to go through life alone. The people we surround ourselves with encourage us (or discourage us) through their actions, goals, and support.

- Find a tribe that'll help you become the best version of yourself. Use your moral compass to align with like-minded people who have backgrounds and experiences you can learn from.

- Focus on being a good member of your tribe. The effort you invest in building these relationships will prove valuable.

11

TAKE TIME TO REST AND SELF-REFLECT

Destroy the idea that you have to be constantly working or grinding in order to be successful. Embrace the concept that rest, recovery, and reflection are essential parts of... a successful and ultimately happy life.

—AUTHOR UNKNOWN (but whoever said it is a damn genius)

AFTER RETURNING HOME FROM A FOUR-MONTH COMBAT deployment in July 2014, I took command of a highly selective and specialized Army troop as part of the first-ever officer exchange. A month later, we conducted a rapid deployment to Iraq—it was my tenth deployment.

There's an iconic scene in *Legends of the Fall* where Colonel Ludlow, played by Anthony Hopkins, thrusts his sword into the earth and walks away from the military out of disgust for how Native Americans were treated. My Colonel Ludlow moment happened a month into the deployment when I informed leadership that I'd be leaving the military. Instead of being driven by the need to stand against some historical injustice, like in the movie, my decision was far less dramatic.

Up until that moment, my seventeen-year military career was going very well; the problem was everything else was falling apart, especially my marriage. As I briefly discussed in Chapter 3, "The Endless Pursuit of Balance," my focus on attaining professional success came at the expense of my emotional and spiritual health—which impacted my family. While I regularly practiced reflection during my career, it was always to become faster, stronger, and more effective on the battlefield. All I wanted to do was deploy to combat zones with the finest warriors in the world and take the fight to the enemy, which I did—until I burnt out. This unbalanced lifestyle brought my career to a screeching halt.

Worn out and lacking a support system, I struggled to adjust to civilian life. During this time, I realized the SEAL Teams were part of my DNA and that leaving such a tight-knit community meant I wasn't only losing a job—I was also losing a big part of my identity. Over the next two years, I worked closely with the fantastic clinical psychologist Dr. Chris Frueh. He helped me reflect on my experiences, rebuild my identity, and capitalize on the lessons I'd learned. While it wasn't easy, this process helped me separate myself from my work, better understand what I value most, and accept that I must never again sacrifice my emotional and spiritual health for any reason.

Like so many people, I never thought burnout could happen to me—I was so very wrong. My experience is a cautionary tale for what happens when you don't rest and self-reflect, but it's also a testament to what happens when you do.

REST FOR THE BODY, MIND, AND SPIRIT

Raise your hand if you've ever heard any of the following expressions:

- Grind every single day.

- Give 110%.

- 24/7/365.

- You can sleep when you're dead.

Most likely, your hand is in the air. We've all heard these types of messages. While they might sound motivational, following them can be a recipe for disaster. Excuse my language, but the "always grinding" mentality is absolute bullshit. It overlooks an essential requirement of life: rest. If you're grinding nonstop, you're not taking time to reflect and learn, which are indispensable parts of the Everyday Warrior process.

Any physical fitness trainer will tell you that overtraining causes tremendous damage. The same is true for our mind and spirit. Without rest, we become disengaged from our goals and relationships—this is known as burnout.

Prolonged exposure to stress results in a person experiencing burnout, which leads to energy depletion and exhaustion, negativity and cynicism, and reduced efficacy. This kind of disengagement is prevalent in the corporate world but is not unique to the private sector. The military is known for pushing limitations. In the years following September 11, 2001, the incessant demands and grueling deployment cycle of the Global War on Terrorism took their toll on the Special Operations community. The nonstop deployments in some of the world's most dangerous and stressful environments impacted these high performers psychologically and physiologically, often manifesting as self-destructive behaviors or severe depression. A person's mind, body, and spirit, no matter how resilient they may be, can only endure stress for so long.

Performing to the best of your abilities requires rest. Physically, rest allows your body to heal by supporting a healthy immune system and regulating your metabolism. Mentally, rest increases your productivity and creativity, decreases stress, and improves concentration and memory. Spiritually, rest gives you time to reflect, be still, and boost your connection with the world around you.

As an Everyday Warrior, knowing when to rest and care for yourself is as important as fighting the battle.

SIGNS YOU NEED TO REST

We live in a hypercompetitive, high-speed world filled with social media noise, the 24/7 news cycle, and countless other distractions—all pulling us away from resting. While society promotes the compulsion to keep going and going, that's not how human beings operate.

The goal of an Everyday Warrior is to sustain optimal performance over time. To accomplish this, you must learn to recognize when your body, mind, and spirit are telling you it's time to rest. Beyond heavy eyelids, frequent yawns, and aching muscles, there are other signs we often miss:

- **You lose focus:** Common signs that you may need to rest include struggling to stay on task, trouble keeping your mind from wandering, and difficulty remembering things.

- **Your productivity nosedives:** We are at peak productivity when we're well rested. So, if you feel your efficiency lagging, don't be too hard on yourself and consider taking a break.

- **You make bad decisions or can't make decisions at all:** Our ability to make sound decisions relies on a well-rested mind. When we need rest, we either act impulsively or are overwhelmed by indecision. Neither are suitable and poor decisions will only hurt you later, so consider resting if you're making poor decisions or are struggling to make even the simplest of decisions.

- **You suddenly have a short fuse:** We lash out at those around us when we've reached our maximum capacity. Think about it: are you more likely to lose your cool first thing when you wake up or at the end of a long, stressful day?

Start paying attention to how you act and think so that you can identify the signs before you hit the point of burnout or breakdown. Pay particular attention to your habits. If there is a sudden change in your routine—like binging on ice cream at 3 a.m., abandoning your hobbies, or mindlessly scrolling social media for hours—a lack of rest could be the problem.

WHAT REST IS AND ISN'T

After a long day, many people "rest" by sitting on the couch, turning on the TV, and scrolling through their phone. While that may seem like rest, it's far from it. Rest allows your body, mind, and spirit to be calm and reflect; what many call "rest" actually keeps the mind wired and constantly moving.

What rest looks like depends on the person. I recommend experimenting to figure out what works best for you. Here are some suggestions:

- **Sleep hygiene:** Turn off blue screens (TV, cell phones, tablets) and relax in a calm environment for thirty to sixty minutes before bed. Getting seven to eight hours of sleep is critical to optimal performance, physically, cognitively, and spiritually.

- **Meditation and deep breathing:** Spend between five and thirty minutes meditating or engaged in deep breathing once or twice each day.

- **Practicing gratitude:** Thank others for their contribution, help, or support. List the things you're grateful for in life, no matter how bad the current situation or circumstances may be.

- **Unplugging:** Set your phone to *do not disturb*, step away from screens, and focus on being present in the moment.

- **Spending time outside:** Sometimes rest is as simple as going outside, sitting in the sun, closing your eyes, breathing deeply, and letting your mind wander.

- **Engaging in a passion:** Dive into something you care deeply about, such as reading, hiking, working on the car, or volunteering. Doing things you genuinely enjoy will help you reset.

Here's the key: you must make time in your busy schedule for rest because it will not just happen on its own. Build it into your goal plan.

There's no denying that life is busy. It can be a challenge to keep things running smoothly. That's why most people keep a daily calendar to schedule workouts, meals, appointments, and sports practices. We plan other important events, so why not schedule our rest periods? Not just the hours we sleep, but other parts of our day designated to slow down and reflect. We need to make rest a priority.

While it's important to recognize the warning signs of a lack of rest, it's better not to wait for it to become an issue. Rest isn't a one-and-done activity. By building it into your daily life, you can maintain optimal performance. Cultivate healthy rest habits and work at sustaining them one step ATTA time.

REST LEADS TO REFLECTION

Aside from the benefits we've already discussed, rest is essential for another critical reason: it's an opportunity to reflect.

Rest and reflection function as a loop. When you rest, you create space for self-reflection, and when you engage in self-reflection, you identify the need for rest.

Self-reflection is a crucial trait of the warrior mindset. People associate soldiers with action, not reflection, but this is a misconception. Reflection is so integral to Special Operations that we've built it into our process. In fact, you already know how: after action reviews. Following every mission—training or combat, successful or failure—we review what happened. This debriefing period allows us to slow down and assess our approach, hold ourselves accountable, identify strengths and weaknesses, and improve.

As an Everyday Warrior, you should also conduct after action reviews. You've already been practicing these throughout the book, and I hope you continue doing them on your own. While reflection can happen at any time, consider incorporating it during these five key moments:

1. **When you start a goal or reach a milestone:**
   For the best chance of success, start every big goal with a period of reflection. Then, each time you reach a milestone, check back in with yourself to ensure your goals are still reasonable, attainable, and in line with your definition of success. Taking time for self-assessment allows you to adapt to the ever-changing situation on the ground.

2. **After mistakes or failures:** While we all make decisions we regret, reflection helps us assess what happened and why. This simple step encourages us to evaluate our choices objectively and break the cycle. Self-assessment sparks insight that spurs positive action. Say that you realize you could have handled a situation better—it's never too late to hold yourself accountable by discussing it with those involved.

3. **Following success:** It's human nature to focus on the negative more than the positive, but we must learn to resist that instinct. Look back at your accomplishments and praise yourself—because you deserve it! Take the time to identify the positive behaviors or actions that led to success and try to replicate them next time.

4. **When you're finally ready:** The time will come when you feel compelled to reflect on things from your past. Lean into it, whether it's been weeks, months, or even years. Sometimes, we must grow before we're ready to learn from an experience. There is no statute of limitations on accountability.

5. **Regularly:** For me, daily reflection is essential. I've developed a routine that includes journaling to begin and end my day (Morning Affirmations and Evening

Reflections)—a positive habit that continues serving me well. While doing this daily may not work for everybody, regular reflection is essential for success. Consider creating a practice that works for you and aligns with your goals.

Living a fulfilling life is about the journey, not the destination. Anthony de Mello's story "The Little Fish," which was featured in Pixar's *Soul*, illustrates this point perfectly: A young fish swims up to an old fish and asks how to get to the ocean. The old fish looks up and says, "The ocean? Well, that's what you're swimming in right now." The young fish shakes his head and says, "No, I'm looking for the ocean...what we're swimming in now is just water." If we make the destination the most important thing, we go through life so focused on the end that we forget to enjoy the journey. Then, when we finally arrive at the place we've been waiting for, it's rarely as great as we imagined it would be. Said another way, if we spend all of our time looking forward to living the life we want, we'll miss the life we have.

So many times, I've achieved an objective and found it didn't give me the feeling or satisfaction that I expected. Then, when I look back at the path that got me there, I see that what I learned along the way sustained me. It's not action or achievement that fulfills us, but the journey. Reflecting on the journey encourages us to focus on what matters—impacting others—and helps us recognize the growth and progress we've made. That's the path to fulfillment—that's our ocean.

After Action Review

- Set aside five to ten minutes at the end of each day to complete a personal after action review (Evening Reflection) and ask yourself:

  * What did I plan for today?

  * What happened according to plan, and what didn't?

  * What did I do well, and what did I do poorly?

  * What did I learn, and what actions must I take to not repeat my mistakes?

  * Did my actions move me closer or further from my goals?

  * How did my actions impact those around me?

- Set aside five to ten minutes at the end of each week to assess your physical, mental, and spiritual fitness. Look toward next week and the steps you must take to improve your overall health, focus, and productivity.

- Choose one day each week to rest and reflect. Limit cell phone use while spending more time outside (active rest), with family and friends (tribe), and doing activities you enjoy. Take an inventory of how you feel and how it impacts your mental and spiritual fitness at the end of the day.

Key Takeaways

- Acknowledge the value of rest. Our bodies, minds, and spirits require periods of rest to sustain our performance and prevent burnout.

- Learn to recognize what rest is and is not. Pay attention to signs that you need rest and engage in activities that replenish you.

- Remember the power of reflection. Reaching our goals is about so much more than the goal itself. By reflecting on our journeys, we grow and progress in ways we might never have anticipated.

CONCLUSION

CONGRATULATIONS, YOU'VE FINISHED THE BOOK—NOW THE hard work begins! It's time to take the principles you learned in each chapter and apply them to your life. Self-help books fail miserably when it comes to helping you turn what you've learned into how you live. Luckily for you, *The Everyday Warrior* isn't a self-help book. It's a guide to living that will help you overcome life's challenges; improve your physical, mental, and spiritual health; and become more resilient. You can do this by making the practices and structures discussed in this book a part of your everyday routine—such as conducting a personal inventory to gauge your growth, using discipline training wheels until you get your balance, or implementing the "Framework for Success" to achieve your goals. This may seem like a lot, but if you look back at the AARs you completed along the way, you'll realize just how much progress you've already made. Keep going!

Everyday Warriors face their daily battles with confidence, bravery, and integrity. They're guided by these eleven fundamental truths that inform their actions and help them live a more fulfilling, purposeful, and impactful life:

1. Establish the mindset of a warrior—hold yourself to high standards.

2. Embrace failure—there's no better motivator or teacher.

3. Strive for balance through mental, physical, and spiritual fitness.

4. Know thyself and continually seek self-improvement (courtesy of the U.S. Marine Corps and Army).

5. Take ownership of your life. You are not a victim.

6. Don't be a spectator; step into the arena of life. Set your intention, form a plan, and take action. Then, reflect and repeat.

7. Don't take shortcuts—they don't work! Live life one step ATTA time.

8. Learn to be comfortable being uncomfortable. Hard choices lead to an easy life.

9. The Warrior Way: Get Shit Done. Make Shit Happen. Do It All Again Tomorrow. These are the hallmarks of discipline and accountability.

10. Find your tribe. Make sure they aspire to be great— iron sharpens iron.

11. Learn to honestly critique yourself, and take time to rest, reflect, and grow.

The truth is, you'll lose more than a few battles in your life— but failure is okay. The only thing that's not okay is giving up. Although life is difficult, you're not alone. That's important to remember because alone, we are warriors; together, we're an army. It's amazing what we can accomplish when we are part of a team.

Do you know what else we have in common? Each of us has the same amount of time in a day: 24 hours = 1,440 minutes = 86,400 seconds. No matter how you measure time, it's always the same. As an Everyday Warrior, there's only one thing you can do with that time:

Get Shit Done. Make Shit Happen. Do It All Again Tomorrow. That's the Warrior Way.

THE EVERYDAY WARRIOR PLEDGE

I PLEDGE TO STRIVE FOR PROGRESS INSTEAD OF PERFECTION, develop a bias for action, and never stop pursuing potential. I commit to a lifelong journey of personal growth and acknowledge that lasting change requires time and consistency—not hacks and shortcuts. I accept that failure is a part of the process and that we learn more from our struggles than our successes. I will fall, but I pledge to always get back up, regroup, and continue moving forward. I will do my best to inspire others through my actions, compassion, and vulnerability—because I am an Everyday Warrior.

ACKNOWLEDGMENTS

THIS BOOK WAS MADE POSSIBLE THROUGH THE CONTRIBU-
tions of countless like-minded military and business leaders
who share a passion for personal development and growth,
leadership, and sharing knowledge to help those around us
succeed, especially the generations to come. To the contributors Brian Gordon, George Silva, and Jason Boulay—this has
been an unforgettable and impactful journey. I couldn't (and
wouldn't) have done it without you guys. I loved the professional, tactful, and sometimes heated debates on what to
include in this book. I'm a better person for having heard each
of your perspectives on life and am grateful for having had the
opportunity to share mine.

To Kelsey Adams, thank you for your patience and mentorship throughout this process...again! I couldn't have written
the first book or this book without your help, and I can't wait
to finish the third book alongside you, Rich Diviney, Brian
Decker, George Randle, and Tom Lokar.

I would also like to thank my wife, Jordan, and the entire Dunagan family. Edmund, Antoinette, Nicole, E.J. Sarraille, and all the delinquents I call nephew and niece. Trey Holder and the Accelerate360 team. The Talent War Group team— George Randle, Karli Waldon, Josh Johnson, Joe McNamara, Lisa Jaster, Michelle Ballesteros, Nayara González, Will Sharman, Wredge, and Migs. The Men's Journal Everyday Warrior team and contributors—James Heidenry, Tom Freestone, Jen Rost, Brittany Smith, Rob Dixter, Rob Jones, Andy Stumpf, Dr. Chris Frueh, Rich Diviney, Elia Saikaly, Nick Shaw, Dr. Kirk Parsley, Gabrielle Lyon, and so many others.

Lastly, to the two people who mean more to me than life itself, my children, Camryn and Caden, I love you beyond words. I couldn't be any prouder of the young woman and young man you've become. My only wish is that you define what success means to you and then pour everything you have into making it a reality. I am always with you.

MEET THE CONTRIBUTORS

GEORGE SILVA

Raised in Krum, Texas, George Silva is the founder of Alpha Mentorship, a company that uses baseball to teach children about life. In 2021, he retired from the Navy after twenty years of service and multiple deployments. George serves as the business manager at 3One Ventures and is an executive search consultant for Talent War Group.

Endless gratitude to my wife, Alicia. Each moment with you never feels long enough, but those moments have brought me more happiness and joy than I could have imagined. To my children, Leevi, Easton, and Cali, I grow prouder of you every day; you inspire me to reach further and aim higher. Thank you to Mike, Jason, and the entire team for an incredible experience.

JASON BOULAY

Jason Boulay is a writer, photographer, and the founder of Ink Slinger Creative, a full-service writing and design agency based in Cranston, Rhode Island. He's also the head of digital media and editorial content writing at Talent War Group and an Army veteran who served in Afghanistan from 2002–2003. Jason graduated from Bryant University in 2015 with a Bachelor of Arts in political science/law and communication.

Thank you to my wife, Melissa. You're my love, best friend, and everything beautiful and good in this world. To my sons, Liam, Jameson, and Luke, words can't express my love for you, the joy you've brought me, or how proud I am to be your dad. To Mike, George, and the team, I am forever grateful to you for bringing me into your tribe.

BRIAN GORDON

A California transplant now living on the Jersey Shore, Brian Gordon has spent twenty years as a successful entrepreneur who founded, ran, and exited two agency service companies. Today, he's the founder and operator of BIG Strategy, an executive consulting agency specializing in business management and marketing strategy.

> *I want to thank my wife, Maria. I've never seen anyone fight harder for their beliefs; you embody the Everyday Warrior mindset and are my inspiration. To my children, Jackson, Lucas, and Benjamin, you're my pride and joy—but also the source of many battles (and I love you for it). To my parents, David and Deborah, thank you for leading by example and showing me what never giving up looks like—you are true Everyday Warriors.*

JOIN OUR TRIBE AND OUR JOURNEY:

https://mikesarraille.com
Instagram: @mr.sarraille

www.talentwargroup.com
LinkedIn: Talent War Group

https://www.mensjournal.com/everyday-warrior/
Instagram: @the_everydaywarrior

LEGACY EXPEDITIONS

https://legacyexpeditions.net
Instagram: @legacyexpeditions